W9-BIX-874

For current pricing information,
or to learn more about this or any Nextext title,
call us toll-free at **1-800-323-5435**
or visit our web site at www.nextext.com.

STORIES IN HISTORY

AMERICA IN CONFLICT

1941-1985

nextext

Cover illustration: Todd Leonardo

Printed in the United States of America

ISBN 0-618-22197-2

1 2 3 4 5 6 7 — QKT — 08 07 06 05 04 03 02

Table of Contents

PART 2: THE COLD WAR

About this Book

The stories are historical fiction. They are based on historical fact, but some of the characters and events may be fictional. In the Sources section, you'll learn which is which, and where the information came from.

The illustrations are all historical. If they are from a time different from the story, the caption tells you. Original documents help you understand the time period. Maps let you know where things were.

Items explained in People and Terms to Know are repeated in the Glossary. Look there if you come across a name or term you don't know.

Historians do not always know or agree on the exact dates of events in the past. The letter c before a date means "about" (from the Latin word circa).

If you would like to read more about these exciting times, you will find recommendations in Reading on Your Own.

Explosions rock Pearl Harbor following the Japanese attack on December 7, 1941. ▶

Background

Yesterday, Dec. 7, 1941—a date which will live in infamy—the United States of America was suddenly and deliberately attacked by naval and air forces of the Empire of Japan.

—President Roosevelt,
describing the attack on Pearl Harbor

World War II

The World Before the War

After World War I, America largely stayed out of the affairs of other nations. This policy of isolationism lasted for more than 20 years. Most Americans wanted to focus on problems at home—such as those of the Great Depression of the 1930s—rather than on events in foreign countries. The United States even refused to be a member of the League of Nations, an international organization founded after World War I. The League's purpose was to keep peace in the world.

However, by the 1930s trouble began to brew in Europe. The dictators of Germany and Italy, Adolf Hitler and Benito Mussolini, raised huge armies. On the other side of the world, Japan moved toward creating a Pacific empire by invading China. During this period, Germany made an alliance with Italy and Japan, forming the Axis powers.

In order to keep peace, England and France did not oppose Hitler at first. This policy only made him bolder. In 1939, he and Soviet dictator Joseph Stalin secretly agreed to divide Poland between them and not to fight each other.

The War in Europe

World War II began on September 1, 1939, when Hitler's troops invaded Poland. Two days later, England and France declared war on Germany. By the spring of 1940, German armies had control of Denmark, Norway, Holland, and Belgium. They

Greatest Extent of Axis Control in World War II

then swept across France, trapping the British army at Dunkirk on the English Channel. A few weeks later, on June 14, Hitler's army occupied Paris. Great Britain faced the Axis powers alone.

In November 1940, Franklin D. Roosevelt was re-elected president of the United States. He had told Americans that he would not send their sons to fight overseas. He would, however, send military supplies to help the British and French. Many Americans wanted their country to join the war. Among them were those who feared that Hitler would kill all of Europe's Jews.

The attack that finally caused America to enter the war came from Japan. On December 7, 1941, Japanese warplanes carried out a surprise attack on the U.S. naval base at Pearl Harbor, Hawaii. They killed more than 2,400 Americans and destroyed much of the U.S. Pacific Fleet. Roosevelt asked Congress to declare war on Japan. By December 11, America was at war with the Axis powers.

Earlier in 1941, Hitler had broken his word to Stalin and invaded the Soviet Union. During this period, the Germans ran concentration camps in which millions of Jews, Poles, Russians, Gypsies, and others were killed. It was a dark moment in human history.

Then, in 1943, the war began to change. Millions of Russians died, but finally the Soviets pushed the Germans out. Later that year, Mussolini resigned, and Italy surrendered. Roosevelt met with the leaders of Great Britain and the Soviet Union to plan "Operation Overlord." This was to be the D-Day invasion of France, which was still occupied by Germany.

The D-Day invasion took place on June 6, 1944. Allied forces stormed ashore on the French beaches at Normandy, under heavy German fire. After sustaining huge losses, the Allies won the day. By October, the Germans had been driven out of France. Germany surrendered to the Allies in May 1945.

The War in the Pacific

While war raged in Europe, Japanese forces were on the march throughout Southeast Asia and the Pacific. By 1942, Japan occupied Korea, Thailand, Singapore, French Indochina, New Guinea, large parts of China, the Philippines, and many other islands in the Pacific.

American morale improved in June 1942. That's when Navy pilots destroyed Japan's main naval force during the Battle of Midway. One by one, the Pacific islands were won back from the Japanese. U.S. General Douglas MacArthur recaptured the Philippines in July 1945.

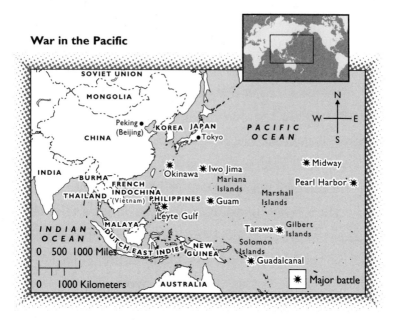

War in the Pacific

During the Battle of Leyte Gulf, the Japanese made suicide "kamikaze" attacks, crashing their planes into American ships. But there was no stopping the American military's advance toward Japan itself. From late 1944 into 1945, American pilots began a series of bombing raids on Japan. Still Japan did not give up.

On August 6, 1945, following orders from President Truman, an American plane dropped an atomic bomb on the Japanese city of Hiroshima. Three days later, a second atomic bomb hit another Japanese city, Nagasaki. These bombings brought horrific death and suffering to Japanese civilians. On August 14, Japan surrendered to the Allies.

The Home Front

World War II brought about many changes on the home front. Many goods were rationed (or in limited supply). These included sugar, coffee, meat, fats and oils, cheese, shoes, and rubber tires. Because so many American men were sent overseas, women filled the jobs they left. During the war years, the number of American women who worked outside their homes increased from about 12 million to about 18.5 million. Many women worked at defense-related factories, in jobs previously held only by men.

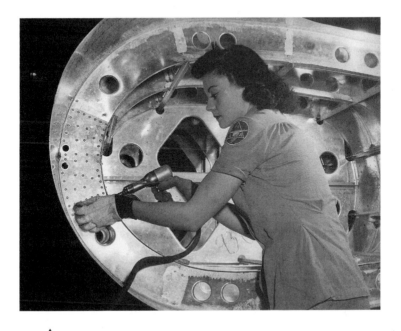

▲
A woman war worker tightens bolts on the fuel tank of a bomber.

While the war often brought out the best in Americans, it also brought out the worst. Americans, angry at Japan because of Pearl Harbor, turned against Japanese Americans, most of whom lived on the West Coast. Fearing that some Japanese Americans might help Japan, Roosevelt ordered the roundup of more than 100,000 Japanese Americans. These families were kept in camps in remote areas of the western United States for the rest of the war.

The Cold War

How the Cold War Began

After the war ended, the Soviet Union took over several Eastern European nations and made them part of the communist system. Although the U.S. and the Soviet Union had been allies during the war, the two nations soon saw each other as a threat. They didn't fight one another directly, but competed fiercely in almost every way. The situation came to be described as a "cold war." For over 40 years, the United States and the Soviet Union built and tested nuclear weapons. It seemed as if a "hot war" could begin at almost any time.

In 1949, the United States and its European allies created the North Atlantic Treaty Organization (NATO). The purpose of this alliance was to protect its members against Soviet attack. That same year, the part of Germany controlled by the Soviets became a communist country. It was now one of many countries in Eastern Europe that were "satellites" of the Soviet Union. An "Iron Curtain," in the words of British leader Winston Churchill, had fallen across Europe. It divided the communist East from the democratic West.

The Korean War

When World War II ended, Korea (which had been occupied by the Japanese) was divided between the United States and the Soviet Union. North Korea became a communist nation. South Korea was ruled by an anticommunist dictator. In 1950, the North Korean army tried to unify all of Korea by invading the South. Soon after, American-led United Nations troops forced North Korea to retreat. America was at war again, just five years after World War II.

General Douglas MacArthur wanted President Truman to allow him to invade North Korea. When

▲

U.S. Marines advance against Chinese forces during the Korean War.

the North Korean army had been pushed almost to the Chinese border, China became alarmed. Suddenly 300,000 Chinese troops swept across the border, where American forces suffered high casualties.

At this point, Truman believed the most sensible plan was to seek a peace agreement that kept the country divided. MacArthur publicly criticized Truman's decision. He even said nuclear weapons should be used. In 1951, Truman fired MacArthur. In 1953, the fighting stopped. Korea has remained divided ever since.

McCarthyism

On February 9, 1950, Joseph McCarthy, a Republican senator from Wisconsin, announced that he had a list of 205 communists who worked in the State Department. But when asked, McCarthy had few details for reporters. His list of 205 names shrank to 57, and then to just 4 names. It was also not clear

▲
Senator Joseph McCarthy goes in front of a TV camera to report his beliefs about communists in the U.S. government.

whether the people named were actually communists, people who somehow helped the cause of communism, or people who agreed with communist ideas.

McCarthy's four-year campaign of accusations and threats spread to people from other walks of life, causing many people to lose their jobs. Because Americans feared communism so much, McCarthy became one of the most powerful men in the land. In 1954, he failed to expose communists he claimed were in the U.S. Army. In these televised Senate hearings McCarthy showed an ugly, cruel side in his treatment of witnesses. Public opinion turned against him. However, the anticommunist crusade he had started continued to influence American society and politics.

World War III?

In 1949, the Soviet Union exploded an atomic bomb. America learned it was no longer the only nation with nuclear weapons. Soon air-raid drills were being conducted across the country. Many Americans were so fearful of nuclear war that they built bomb shelters in their backyards.

The United States and the Soviet Union became involved in a dangerous arms race. Both nations rushed to test more powerful nuclear bombs and missiles. In 1950, the United States started work on a hydrogen bomb thousands of times more powerful than the atomic bomb. Before long, both countries had stores of enough nuclear weapons to wipe each other out completely. This policy was known as M. A. D.—"Mutual Assured Destruction." Both sides would be destroyed if either side was foolish enough to start a nuclear war.

▲

The United States and the Soviet Union climb a giant A (for atomic weapons) towards an unknown future. This political cartoon expressed the fears of many Americans about the arms race.

In 1957, the Soviet Union launched *Sputnik I.* It was the world's first man-made satellite to go into orbit around the earth. Many Americans reacted with shock and outrage. Would the Soviet Union be able to launch nuclear missiles at the United States from space? The American government immediately began pouring money into space research.

Tensions increased sharply in the fall of 1962. A U.S. spy plane took photos of Soviet missile bases in Cuba, an island nation near Florida. President John F. Kennedy knew that missiles launched from Cuba could easily strike cities in the United States. On October 22, his televised speech told Americans about the missiles in Cuba. He demanded their removal and announced that American ships would prevent Soviet ships from bringing more missiles.

Many people thought World War III—a nuclear war—was about to begin. Fortunately, Soviet leader Nikita Khrushchev was not eager to start a nuclear war. The Soviets agreed to take their missiles out of Cuba and tear down the launch sites. The United States agreed not to invade Cuba.

The Vietnam Era

How the Vietnam War Began

During the Cold War, American policy makers believed that if one country fell under communist control, nearby countries would also fall. That is how the United States became involved in Vietnam.

When Vietnam won independence from France in 1954, the country was divided much like Korea had been, with the communists in the north. When communist forces in South Vietnam began fighting the South Vietnamese government in 1960, they received assistance from North Vietnam. The United States then sent South Vietnam several hundred military advisors.

The War Expands

In 1964, President Lyndon Johnson reported North Vietnamese attacks on U.S. naval vessels in the Gulf of Tonkin, near Vietnam. Congress then allowed Johnson to do what was necessary to protect American troops. The Johnson administration was certain that the South Vietnamese would never be able to win the war against the communists by itself. Johnson ordered more troops to Vietnam. By 1965,

▲

U.S. paratroopers patrol Phuoc Tuy province in South Vietnam in 1966.

many American servicemen were dying in the jungles of Vietnam. In 1967, the Air Force flew more than 800 bombing raids a month, but caused little damage to North Vietnam's war effort.

The Home Front

Throughout the early part of the war, most Americans supported U.S. policy in Vietnam. Government leaders assured the nation that America was winning the war and that the end was in sight. However, as the war continued, growing numbers of Americans came to view their nation's policies regarding Vietnam as wrong. Each day, television viewers saw young American soldiers being wounded and killed. Thousands of people began to protest the war in city streets.

The deep divisions among Americans because of the Vietnam War would take many years to heal. Some people blamed antiwar protesters for America's loss in the war. And the protesters blamed the government for the deaths of more than 58,000 young Americans.

Withdrawal from Vietnam

In early 1968 North Vietnam launched a major surprise attack against South Vietnam's cities. It came to be called the "Tet Offensive." Although the North Vietnamese were eventually driven back, they had reached targets in the South Vietnamese capital of Saigon and other large cities. According to a survey, 60 percent of the American public believed the Tet offensive was a defeat for South Vietnam. It now seemed that the war could not be won.

War in Vietnam

Richard Nixon became President after Johnson in 1969, but did no better in the war effort. National Security Advisor Henry Kissinger began secret talks with the North Vietnamese. In 1973, a peace agreement was signed, and American troops left South Vietnam. Fighting continued until April 1975, when the North Vietnamese united the country once again.

Legacy of Vietnam

Sadly, the veterans of the war, for the most part, were not welcomed as heroes upon their return to the U.S. Because of their wartime experiences, many would face great difficulties coping with life in America.

To honor the memory of American soldiers who had sacrificed their lives for their country, Maya Lin, an American sculptor and architect, was hired to design the Vietnam Veterans Memorial in Washington, D.C. The Wall, as it is called, has become a national shrine. Those visiting it—Vietnam veterans, their loved ones, and others—are deeply moved by the experience.

Time Line

1939—World War II begins in Europe.

1941—Japan attacks Pearl Harbor; U.S. enters World War II.

1944—D-Day; Allies invade Europe at Normandy.

1945—Germany and Japan surrender.

1950—Korean War begins.

1953—Korean War cease-fire is agreed to.

1954—Senator Joseph McCarthy claims communist influence in U.S. Army.

1957—Soviet Union launches *Sputnik 1*.

1962—Soviet Union places nuclear missiles in Cuba.

1965—First U.S. ground troops go to Vietnam.

1968—Vietcong launch Tet Offensive.

1973—U.S. involvement in Vietnam War ends.

1975—South Vietnam surrenders to communists.

1982—Vietnam Veterans Memorial is dedicated.

World War II

An American Family Learns of Pearl Harbor

BY WALTER HAZEN

I remember the day as if it were yesterday. Although I was only seven at the time, the events of Sunday, December 7, 1941, are in my mind forever.

It was shortly after one o'clock in the afternoon. My brother and I had just finished lunch and were kicking a football back and forth in the yard. We were laughing and roughhousing and having a good time. Thoughts of war were far from our minds. Suddenly my mother came running from the house. The look on her face told us that something terrible had happened.

The script of a news report on Pearl Harbor shows the announcer's markings for emphasis. An index card listing NBC's news broadcasts for December 7 includes the break in regularly scheduled programming to announce news of the attack.

"**Pearl Harbor**!" she cried. "Pearl Harbor! The Japanese have bombed Pearl Harbor!"

Well, we boys had no idea where Pearl Harbor was or even *what* it was. From watching the **newsreels** at the old Isis Theater in town, we knew that the Japanese had invaded a place called **French Indochina** a few months earlier. But that didn't mean anything to us either. As far as we knew, French Indochina might have been on the Moon. So when Mom ran into the yard all beside herself, we had no idea what she was hollering about.

For the rest of that afternoon we sat huddled around the radio.

For the rest of that afternoon we sat huddled around the radio. We couldn't move as more details of the attack came in. My sister Betty, who was at a friend's house when the news broke, hurried home on her bicycle to join us. At 13 years old, she was almost twice my age, and she understood

---

People and Terms to Know

Pearl Harbor—major U.S. naval base near Honolulu, Hawaii. Japanese planes made a surprise attack on it on December 7, 1941, that brought the United States into World War II.

newsreels—short films covering recent news events. Newsreels were shown in theaters, usually before the main movie.

French Indochina—area of southeast Asia once controlled by France. Today the region includes the nations of Laos (LAH•ohs), Cambodia, and Vietnam. See the map on page 26.

---

the seriousness of the situation. She took her place near the radio and tried not to show us how frightened she was.

(Betty didn't fool me, however. I knew that when she was nervous or worried about something she bit her fingernails. At that moment, she was gnawing away like a beaver!)

My mother was worried about Dad. He was stationed aboard an **aircraft carrier** that was based at Pearl Harbor. Was the carrier in port at the time? Was it at sea? The look on Mom's face told me that she feared the worst.

The first news of the attack had come at exactly 2:26 P.M., Eastern Standard Time. This meant it was 1:26 P.M. in Pensacola, Florida, my hometown. My mother had the radio on as she ironed clothes, half listening to a professional football game being played in New York. Suddenly the game was interrupted with this announcement:

People and Terms to Know

aircraft carrier—warship with a flat deck from which fighter planes can take off and land. Aircraft carriers are necessary because such planes often cannot hold enough fuel for long flights.

Ladies and gentlemen, we interrupt this broadcast to bring you an important bulletin from the United Press. Flash! Washington—The White House announces a Japanese attack on Pearl Harbor! Stay tuned for further developments to be broadcast as they are received!

▲
A small boat rescues a crewman from the burning U.S.S. *West Virginia.*

Mom told us this as she strained to hear additional news that was coming in. Too young to realize our timing was bad, we immediately began pestering her with questions.

"Where is Pearl Harbor?"

"Is Daddy there?"

"Do you think he's all right?"

"Did he shoot down any planes?"

"Will he be coming home for Christmas?"

How did the Japanese get all the way to Pearl Harbor and still get home afterwards?

That last question did it. My sister gave each of us a look that told us we'd best shut up. When we continued, Mom exploded.

"Betty," she shouted, "take your brothers outside and keep them there! I can't hear myself think!"

Betty whisked us out the front door and into the yard. I understand now that we were getting on Mom's nerves, but at the time I was angry and hurt. I must admit that I was probably more concerned with Christmas and presents under the tree than I was with my Dad's safety. Maybe that's because I understood so little about the attack that I tried not to think about it. Thinking about things I didn't understand just made me frustrated.

For example, I looked at a map and saw that Japan was nowhere near Hawaii. In fact, it was almost 4,000 miles away! How did the Japanese get all the way to Pearl Harbor and still get home afterwards? Betty, annoyed, told me that's what aircraft carriers were for—didn't I know that? Well, that made me confused about something else. Aircraft carriers are huge, bigger than football fields. How could they sneak up on us? How could America be so unprepared?

Betty didn't have a fast answer to this question, though. The leaders of the United States didn't either. It took a long time for all the facts to come out, and some weren't known until long after the war. It turned out that the U.S. ambassador in Tokyo *had* been warning that Japan might attack suddenly just like it had done in earlier wars. And some folks in Washington, D.C., after getting hold of Japanese secret messages, had been expecting an attack somewhere for weeks. The problem was, they didn't know where it would take place.

Several days passed before my family learned all the details about Pearl Harbor, but we found out some things pretty quickly. Planes from six Japanese aircraft carriers took off when their ships were about 275 miles north of the Hawaiian island of <u>Oahu</u>. They came in two waves. The first wave

---

People and Terms to Know

Oahu—third largest and most important of the Hawaiian Islands. Honolulu, Hawaii's largest city, is located on Oahu.

came over Pearl Harbor and nearby bases and airfields at 7:55 in the morning, Hawaii time. They bombed the airfields first, and we later found out that they destroyed 188 of our planes and damaged 159 others. That done, they turned their attention to eight American battleships lined up neatly at Pearl Harbor. They had hoped that three of our aircraft carriers, one of which was my Dad's, would be anchored there along with the battleships. By a stroke of luck, the carriers were at sea on a training mission. Those carriers would later play a major role in our winning the war.

A second wave of Japanese planes came in at 8:54. By that time, our airfields and the ships in the harbor were ablaze. In less than two hours, the Japanese struck all eight of our battleships. Two, the *Arizona* and the *Oklahoma*, sank and were lost. Several others sank but were later repaired and went back into action. In addition, ten other ships were either sunk or disabled.

As we listened to further radio broadcasts, I could see my mother's concern grow. I don't think she slept at all until several days later, when the telephone rang. It was Dad!

"Your Daddy's OK," she said as she hung up the phone and hugged us, tears streaming down her face. "His ship was out at sea when it happened."

"Will he be coming home soon?" I asked, jumping up and down. "Will he be here for Christmas?"

"Not hardly," she answered. "He might not be coming home for a long, long time. Right now, his country needs him more than we do. But he's safe. That's the important thing."

More than 2,400 Americans were killed at Pearl Harbor.

We, of course, were happy and relieved. But for many American families, the Japanese attack brought pain and suffering. More than 2,400 Americans were killed at Pearl Harbor. Another 1,200 were wounded. Of those killed, almost half died when the *Arizona* blew up and sank. Today there's a memorial to those fallen Americans right out in the water. Underneath the memorial you can see the *Arizona* just below the surface.

The day after the attack, President **Franklin Roosevelt** asked for and received from Congress a declaration of war against Japan. Three days later, Japan's **allies**, Germany and Italy, declared war on

---

People and Terms to Know

Franklin Roosevelt—(1882–1945) 32nd president of the United States, elected first in 1932 and then three times after that. He helped the country get through both the Great Depression and most of World War II.

allies—countries joined together for a common purpose, such as defeating an enemy.

the United States. After that, we were in for four long years of fighting.

I remember asking my mother on several occasions why the Japanese had bombed Pearl Harbor. Each time, she would only shrug, shake her head, and say something like "I wish I knew." Many weeks passed before we learned that Japan's goal was to destroy the U.S. Pacific Fleet. With the U.S. fleet out of the way, there would be nothing to stop Japan from taking control of all of southeast Asia.

I grew up a lot during those four years we were at war. From a little boy more concerned with Christmas presents than anything else, I grew into a young person who gradually understood what was taking place. And, as I said at the beginning of my story, I shall never forget what happened that day in December 1941. It was, as President Roosevelt said before Congress the following day, "a date which will live in infamy." That means it was shameful and disgraceful on a large scale. Well, no one can deny that. But the attack also became the rallying cry for our nation. "Remember Pearl Harbor!" people would exclaim. It was like saying, "We didn't start this war, but we're the ones who are going to finish it."

QUESTIONS TO CONSIDER

1. How did the narrator learn about the attack on Pearl Harbor?

2. What did the narrator do that shows that he did not really understand what was taking place?

3. How were Japanese planes able to reach Hawaii, which is nearly 4,000 miles from Japan?

4. How could the damage suffered by the U.S. Navy at Pearl Harbor have been much worse?

5. Why did Japan think it was necessary to destroy the U.S. Pacific Fleet?

6. Why do you think the words "Remember Pearl Harbor!" became a rallying cry for the United States?

Rosie the Riveter

BY JUDITH CONAWAY

"**P**lease pass the potatoes," said Hannah Johansson. Her brother Joe reached for the bowl. At that exact moment, during an ordinary Sunday dinner, the lives of the Johansson family changed forever.

The radio stopped its music right in the middle of a song. The family sat in stunned silence as they heard the terrifying news. Early that morning, Japanese fighter planes had attacked the American naval base at Pearl Harbor, Hawaii. Several battleships had been lost. **Casualties** were believed to number in the thousands.

People and Terms to Know

Casualties—people killed or wounded.

The next day, December 8, 1941, the United States declared war on Japan. That same week, Hannah's brother Joe joined the United States Navy.

That was Hannah's senior year in high school. She and her friends went to class as usual, but all they could talk about was the war. After they graduated, almost all the boys in the class **enlisted**. Across the country, thousands of boys were doing the same.

The United States was not fully prepared for the fighting. The nation's factories had to work nonstop to make enough planes, ships, weapons, and supplies to win the war. Because so many men had gone off to fight, there was not enough manpower. The factories began asking for womanpower instead. Hannah was eager work in a factory, too, but her parents didn't want her to leave home.

The **Battle of Midway** changed their minds. The battle was an important victory for the United States. But a few days later the Johanssons got word that Joe was **missing in action**.

People and Terms to Know

enlisted—signed up voluntarily to serve in the army, navy, or other branches of the armed services.

Battle of Midway—naval battle that took place near the Midway Islands in the central Pacific, on June 3–6, 1942. It was an important early victory for the United States in the war against Japan.

missing in action—official term for a military person who cannot be accounted for after a battle.

"I have to work—for Joe's sake," Hannah said. Her parents agreed to let her go.

The very next month, Hannah reported to the Richmond Shipyards. These were a chain of seven shipyards built in Richmond, California, at the start of the war. During the next three years she worked harder than she would have believed possible. She saved enough money to start her college career. And she learned firsthand the difference between popular songs and reality.

"I have to work— for Joe's sake," Hannah said.

All the day long,
Whether rain or shine,
She's a part of the __assembly line__.
She's making history,
Working for victory,
__Rosie the Riveter__.

People and Terms to Know

assembly line—arrangement in which products are put together in stages as they pass from worker to worker or machine to machine, often on a conveyor belt.

Rosie the Riveter—imaginary heroine used by the United States during World War II to encourage women to work in war industries. The song "Rosie the Riveter" was written by Redd Evans and John Jacob Loeb.

▲

A group of women assembles an airplane fuselage.

Hannah worked on an assembly line for small engines. The work wasn't hard, but it was boring and tiring. She did the same thing thousands of times a day. Her muscles ached, and her feet were tired. She had headaches too. The noise and heat inside the plant were incredible.

*Keeps a sharp lookout for **sabotage**,*
*Sitting up there on the **fuselage**,*
That little girl can do more than a male will do.

People and Terms to Know

sabotage (SAB•oh•tahj)—destruction of machinery and equipment by enemy agents.
fuselage (FYOO•suh•lahj)—body of an airplane, without its wings, tail, or engines.

No matter what the song said, Hannah and the other "Rosies" were not treated equally on the job. The men on the job teased them and played practical jokes. Some men even tried to sabotage the women's work, to make the Rosies look bad.

The women learned to stick together and to help each other out. Since Hannah was good with tools, she often showed the others what to do. In spite of all they were up against, the women performed as well as the men.

When they gave her a production "E,"
She was as proud as she could be.
There's something true about,
Red, white, and blue about
Rosie the Riveter.

Hannah's boss was no help. He believed that women should not be allowed to take men's jobs, war or no war. When the men made rude comments, the boss did nothing to stop them. On some days, Hannah could hardly bring herself to go to work. She would remember Joe, and remind herself that her country needed her. But the boss still made her mad.

One day in February 1943, the manager called Hannah's boss into his office. The boss came out a few minutes later, looking ten years older. Unable to keep back tears, he told them that his son had been killed at **Guadalcanal**.

Every day there were new reasons to believe or to despair.

The boss went right back to work, and never spoke of his son again. He never made fun of the Rosies again, either. Sometimes, when she saw the heartbroken look on his face, Hannah found herself wishing the boss was still his mean old self.

The shipyard workers knew they were all in this war together. Most of them had brothers, cousins, boyfriends, or husbands in uniform. The war was on everyone's mind, all the time. Every day there were new reasons to believe or to despair.

During 1943, Americans had more and more reasons to hope that they would win the war. German troops finally failed in their long **siege** of

---

People and Terms to Know

Guadalcanal—one of the Solomon Islands in the South Pacific, where several battles were fought between August 1942 and February 1943. The United States and its allies defeated Japanese forces, but at the cost of thousands of lives.

siege—attempt by an army to force a city to surrender by surrounding it and cutting off supplies.

Stalingrad, Russia. Early in March, **Allied** ships and planes won the Battle of the Bismarck Sea in the South Pacific. In May, the **Axis** forces were defeated in North Africa.

In August, Hannah got a new job as a welder. Welders join pieces of metal by heating them until they melt and then pressing the melted pieces together. This job was even hotter, noisier, and more uncomfortable than the assembly line, but Hannah loved it. It was the "real war work" she had signed up to do. Now Hannah spent her days inside the huge ships, sealing every seam tight. She liked to imagine that each ship was the one that would find Joe or bring him home.

Hannah knew that Joe might very well be dead. Maybe they would never know what had happened to him. But the Allies were starting to find Japanese prison camps. So Joe might still be alive.

This hope kept Hannah working hard. The others at the shipyards worked with the same dedication.

Hannah and the other Rosies didn't leave the war behind when they left work. Because food was only available as **rations**, they bought their groceries with tickets. They struggled to find day care for their children. It was especially hard to find decent places to live. There was a terrible shortage of housing. Hannah shared a tiny apartment with two other young women.

On their days off, Hannah and her friends did volunteer work at the **USO** and other servicemen's clubs. They worked at snack counters. They signed up as "pen pals" to write to men on active duty. They danced with hundreds of soldiers and sailors.

Guys proposed to Hannah almost every weekend. It was romantic and fun, but terribly sad, too, because she knew some of these boys would never come back.

To Hannah's great joy, her brother did make it back home. Allied troops found Joseph Johansson

---

People and Terms to Know

rations—specific amounts of food or another valuable item that is allowed to each person or family during wartime. Many everyday items were rationed during World War II so that those in the military would have enough supplies to fight.

USO—(United Service Organizations) volunteer group that provides clubs, entertainment, and other services for men and women in the U.S. armed forces.

in a prisoner of war camp on the **Marshall Islands** in February of 1944. Joe was barely alive—but he had survived.

Hannah kept working until May 1945. She lost her job right after **V-E Day**. By that time thousands of men were flooding back from the war. Factory jobs became "men's work" once more. Most Rosies went back to "women's work" at home.

Nothing in her life made her prouder than the years she had spent in the shipyard.

Hannah went to college instead. She started soon after **V-J Day**. A few years later she became the first woman lawyer in her hometown. She had a long and successful career, a happy marriage, three children, and six grandchildren.

But nothing in her life made her prouder than the years she had spent in the shipyard, serving her country as "Rosie the Riveter."

People and Terms to Know

Marshall Islands—small group of islands in the central Pacific Ocean. They were captured by the United States and its allies during February 1944.

V-E Day—"Victory in Europe" Day on May 8, 1945. President Truman made it a national holiday after Germany surrendered on May 7.

V-J Day—"Victory in Japan" Day on August 15, 1945. This was the day after Japan surrendered, ending World War II.

QUESTIONS TO CONSIDER

1. Why did the Battle of Midway change Hannah's parents' minds about letting her work?

2. Who or what was "Rosie the Riveter"?

3. How would you explain the difference between Rosie's life in the song and Hannah's experiences?

4. How did World War II affect the everyday lives of women and their families?

5. What happened to women workers after World War II ended?

Rosie the Riveter

All the day long, whether rain or shine,
She's a part of the assembly line.
She's making history, working for victory,
       Rosie the Riveter.

Keeps a sharp lookout for sabatoge,
Sitting up there on the fuselage.
That little girl will do more than a male will do.
       Rosie the Riveter.

    Rosie's got a boyfriend, Charlie.
    Charlie, he's a Marine.
    Rosie is protecting Charlie,
    Working overtime on the riveting machine.

When they gave her a production "E,"
She was as proud as she could be.
There's something true about, red, white,
    and blue about,
       Rosie the Riveter.

Navajo Code Talkers

BY JUDITH LLOYD YERO

When we studied World War II, our teacher promised us that a special person would come to talk to us about the war. But when that person walked through the door of the classroom, I couldn't believe my eyes. It was my own grandfather! He had on a soldier's cap and a shirt with military patches. And around his neck was a big medal hung on a necklace of **Navajo** beads.

"Class, this is Mr. Benjamin Chee. He's here today to tell us about a part of the war that we don't find in many textbooks. Mr. Chee was a Navajo **code talker.**"

People and Terms to Know

Navajo—group of Native Americans living in the southwestern United States. A code based on the Navajo language was very important to the United States in its fight against the Japanese in World War II.

code talker—U.S. Marine in the Pacific during World War II whose duty was to transmit important messages in code.

American Indian Marines serving in the Pacific send a message in code based on the Navajo language.

Everyone started asking questions at once. "What's a code talker?" "What's the medal for?"

Grandpa Ben smiled and promised that he'd answer all of our questions. Grandpa spoke in Navajo like all of our teachers. We all spoke English, but talked in Navajo whenever we were with other **Diné**.

Grandpa began by asking us what we knew about the war against the Japanese. We knew that a lot of the fighting had taken place on islands in the Pacific Ocean.

"Yes," said Grandpa. "And when our soldiers landed on those islands, they had no way to get information or orders to one another without the Japanese picking up their radio signals. Many of the Japanese had gone to school in America and spoke better English than the American soldiers."

"Then a young man named Philip Johnson had an idea. Because his father was a **missionary**, Philip had been raised on a **reservation**. He was one of

---

People and Terms to Know

Diné (dee•NAY)—term used by the Navajo to describe their own people.

missionary—religious teacher who works to spread his or her religion to a new country or people where it is not widely known or practiced.

reservation—land set aside by the U.S. government for Native American groups.

very few **Anglos** who could speak and understand the Navajo language."

We all laughed. Some of our Anglo friends say we sound like we're choking to death when we talk.

> *Our language sounds like grunts and gurgles to them.*

Our language sounds like grunts and gurgles to them. I told my friend Charlie that we didn't have as many words to learn because Navajo combines words to make pictures. For example, the word for shoes is *ké*. The word for tires is *chidi' bi'ké*—shoes for a car. Makes perfect sense to us!

"Johnson convinced the generals that the Japanese would never understand military messages if the Navajo language was used as code. Messages were always encoded first. That means they were put into symbols or sounds that can't easily be understood by others. After they're sent, someone at the other end had to decode them back into the original words. Well, Johnson set up tests

People and Terms to Know

Anglos—informal term for white Americans who are not of Hispanic descent.

and proved that we Navajos could encode, transmit, and decode a three-line English message in twenty seconds. The machines they used for the same job took more than half an hour."

"But couldn't the Japanese just get some Navajos of their own to listen in?" asked Katie.

Grandpa Ben shook his head. "Even if a Navajo would have done that, it wouldn't have worked. We didn't just talk to one another—we made up a code. There are no words like "submarine" or "fighter plane" in Navajo, so we made up Navajo words for them. For example, *besh-lo* (iron fish)

This Marine served as a sniper and scout in addition to sending coded messages in Navajo. ▶

meant submarine. *Dah-htih-hi* (hummingbird) meant fighter plane. Only someone trained in the code could understand it—and then, only if he understood Navajo."

"But what if you didn't have a word for something that you had to say?" asked Eddie.

"Then we spelled it out," answered Grandpa Ben. "We kept switching back and forth between English letters and Navajo words. For example, if we needed an 'a', we'd say *wol-la-chee* (ant), *be-la-sana* (apple), or *tse-nill* (axe). Even Navajo soldiers who weren't code-talkers wouldn't know what you were talking about if they heard *tsah* (needle) *wol-la-chee* (ant) *ah-keh-di-glini* (victor) *tash–as–zih* (yucca)."

"NAVY!" we yelled.

Grandpa laughed. "Right—you would have made good code talkers. At the end, we had more than 400 words that were used in most messages, so we didn't need to spell out too many words. That took too much time. If you spent too much time on the radio, the Japanese could track your signal and fire at your position."

"Were there a lot of code talkers, Mr. Chee?"

"Between 1942 and 1946, there were about 400 in all. But we started with 30 in the first group who made up the original code. It wasn't easy. We had to take the same training as the rest of the Marines, so our nights were spent memorizing the code and practicing."

"How did the other soldiers treat you?"

"Pretty good," said Grandpa. "Some of them called us Chief or **Geronimo**, but before long they figured out we were saving their necks. One time, American cannons were firing on our own men. The signalman kept radioing the guns to stop firing on us, but the Americans thought he was really a Japanese trying to trick them.

"We had to take the same training as the rest of the Marines."

Finally, they said, 'Do you have a Navajo?' When I got on the radio and started talking, they finally stopped shooting."

"Once in a while, our soldiers who didn't know us would think we were Japanese dressed as Americans and would take us prisoner. The officers finally assigned an Anglo Marine to travel around with us so we'd be safe."

People and Terms to Know

Geronimo—(c. 1829–1909) Native American who led Apaches to escape their reservations in Arizona in the late 1800s.

Mrs. Benally, our teacher, told us that one Marine major said that if it hadn't been for the Navajo, the Americans would never have taken **Iwo Jima**. She read us a quote from a newspaper during the war. "For three years, wherever the Marines landed, the Japanese got an earful of strange gurgling noises . . . with other sounds resembling the call of a **Tibetan** monk and the sound of a hot water bottle being emptied."

That really got us laughing. Mrs. Benally asked Grandpa to tell us why so few people knew about the code talkers.

"Even after the war, the Japanese still hadn't figured out the code we were using. We were all sworn to secrecy. When we came home and our relatives had an **Enemyway** for us, we couldn't even tell them everything that had happened. It wasn't until 1969 that the code talkers were officially recognized. That's when we were given these medals."

People and Terms to Know

Iwo Jima—(EE•whoh JEE•muh) island in the western Pacific that was under Japanese control until 1945. The United States wanted it as a base for planes bombing Japan. The two sides fought for nearly a month before the United States captured the island.

Tibetan (tih•BEHT•an)—from the Asian country of Tibet, which is now controlled by China.

Enemyway—Navajo ceremony for men who return from battle. It is designed to free them from the spirits of the enemies and the bad memories of battle, bringing them back into harmony with nature.

We all crowded around to see what was on the medal. On the left side, there was an Indian in hunting clothes riding on a horse. On the right side was a picture of the soldiers raising the American flag on Iwo Jima. "What does it mean?" we asked.

"One of the men who raised that flag was **Ira Hayes**, a Native American. Someone painted a picture in his honor—it looked like this medal. The people who had the medals made for us thought that it was a good way to honor Indian Marines."

"It's almost time for Mr. Chee to go, class. We just have time for one more question."

Jimmy raised his hand. He had a serious look on his face. "Mr. Chee? Mrs. Benally told us that back when the war started, the Navajo couldn't even vote in American elections. How come so many Navajos were willing to help the Anglos protect their country?"

Grandpa looked just as serious as Jimmy. "We weren't fighting for *their* country, son. We were fighting for *our* country."

People and Terms to Know

Ira Hayes—(1923–1955) Pima Indian Marine who was one of the men in the famous picture of the American flag being raised on Iwo Jima.

QUESTIONS TO CONSIDER

1. Why did the Marines need the Navajo when they fought the Japanese?

2. What kinds of messages do you think soldiers have to send and receive when they are in battle?

3. Why couldn't the code talkers tell their relatives what they had done?

4. Why do you think the code talkers had three different words for each letter of the alphabet?

5. What do you think Mr. Chee meant when he said, "We weren't fighting for *their* country, son. We were fighting for *our* country"?

D-Day

BY STEPHEN FEINSTEIN

Tension—and fear—filled the air. Private Roger Curran huddled against the wind with fellow soldiers on deck of the **LST**. Roger's LST and about 5,000 other warships and landing craft plowed through the cold water of the **English Channel** toward **Normandy**. The sea was crowded with ships carrying tanks and roughly 175,000 American, British, and Canadian troops. It was **D-Day**, June 6, 1944.

People and Terms to Know

LST—short for "landing ship, tank." These ships were made to carry battle tanks and heavy rolling equipment over sea to battle areas and unload directly onto the shore.

English Channel—body of water that separates England from France.

Normandy—region in northwestern France along the Atlantic coast. The Allies considered it the best place to begin retaking France from German forces.

D-Day—(from the word "designated" plus "day") June 6, 1944, the day chosen for the Allied invasion of Normandy, France, to begin.

American soldiers wade from a landing barge toward the beach at Normandy on D-Day, June 6, 1944.

<u>Operation Overlord</u>, the largest seaborne invasion in history, was about to begin.

The Germans had long known that an Allied invasion of France was coming. They thought the most likely location was Calais, a French town only 20 miles from England, and placed most of their troops there. But the Normandy coast was another possibility. So the Germans constructed the "Atlantic Wall"—a kind of protective fort all along the coast. They placed mines in the sea and on the beaches. They built steel and concrete walls on the beaches and hillsides. Though German forces were stretched thin along the Normandy coast, they were in concrete bunkers with walls three feet thick on the cliffs above the beaches. Armed with machine guns, rocket launchers, and cannons, they waited for the Allies.

Like other young Americans in his regiment, eighteen-year-old Roger had been drafted into the army right out of high school. Roger planned to go to college. But his country was at war and college

People and Terms to Know

Operation Overlord—Allied invasion of France, which had been under Germany's rule for four years. It was led by U.S. General Dwight D. Eisenhower.

would have to wait. As dawn approached, Roger wondered if he would ever see his family again. He wanted to do his part. But in truth, he wished he were anywhere but here.

Roger looked on, helpless, as Loomis fell between the two boats.

$\mathbf{A}$t around 3:00 A.M., the men lowered small, specially designed landing craft into the water. They threw rope nets over the sides of the mother ship. "Here we go," Roger thought. His weapons, ammunition, food and water, and boots weighed heavily on him. He climbed over the side and struggled down the ropes.

With each swell of the sea, the landing craft below him rose up and fell about ten feet. Roger timed his jump from the rope net into the little boat when it was closest to him. His buddy Loomis wasn't so lucky. Roger looked on, helpless, as Loomis fell between the two boats. Loomis screamed when the landing craft slapped against the mother ship, crushing one of his legs.

A group of thirty men and two officers were jammed together on each landing craft. Cold spray from the waves kept hitting Roger in the face. The little boats bobbed up and down, causing many soldiers to become seasick.

Roger was part of the first wave of invaders to go ashore at **Omaha Beach**. He knew they had the toughest job of all: capturing the beach and hills from the Germans. But Roger—cold and wet and seasick—thought it might be a relief to step onto the beach. "If I'm careful," he thought, "I'll be okay." He knew some guys would die on the beach—but not him.

At about 5:20, when light first rose in the east, Roger heard the roar of German anti-aircraft guns. He guessed that Allied planes had begun bombing the Normandy coast. The planners of the D-Day invasion knew that their troops would come under heavy German fire. Allied warplanes were scheduled to bomb the coastline before the troops landed to reduce the German danger. Soon German guns began firing on the Allied fleet. The battleships returned fire, lighting up the sky. To

---

People and Terms to Know

Omaha Beach—one of five beaches along the Normandy coast code-named by the Allies. D-Day invasion forces landed here and on Utah, Gold, Juno, and Sword beaches.

Roger, it was the most amazing fireworks display he'd ever seen.

Roger expected that they would hit the beach in about an hour, and finish off what the flyboys had started. Meanwhile, the **LCTs** began launching their tanks. At 6:30, the first American tank on Omaha Beach fired at a German gun and silenced it. When Roger's boat touched sand, the ramp went down. Lieutenant Purvis shouted, "Move, you guys, move!" At that moment, German machine gunners, hiding in **pillboxes** on the beach, opened fire. Bullets tore through Lt. Purvis's body, and he fell dead into the water.

Roger and several others also fell into the water. They were alive, but Roger wondered how long that would last. His heavy equipment dragged him under the water. He struggled to come up, and for a second he thought he might drown. Then he felt a pair of strong arms pull him up. They belonged to Joe Salerno, a fun-loving "tough guy" from the

---

People and Terms to Know

LCTs—short for "landing craft, tank," a tank-carrying landing craft, much smaller than an LST.

pillboxes—small, low concrete structures on which machine guns and anti-tank weapons can be placed.

Bronx, New York. Together they splashed through the water to the shore. All around them shells exploded. Lifeless bodies floated in seawater turning red with blood.

All around them shells exploded.

The machine-gun fire on the beach had not stopped. Roger and Joe immediately hit the ground. Bullets whizzed in from all directions. Just ahead was a steel obstacle. A voice behind them yelled, "Move it up, get behind that steel!" It was Sergeant Weinberg, who was now in command. He inched along the sand on his belly. Joe joined him, and together they took shelter behind the steel.

"Come on, Roger!" yelled Joe. Roger couldn't move. White-faced and wide-eyed, he had never been so scared. A shell exploded on his right, and a soldier named Collins used his left hand to hold what remained of his right arm. Nothing in Roger's training had prepared him for such horror. Finally, Roger got control of himself and crawled towards Joe and Weinberg.

There was no letup of the German fire. Unfortunately, the Allied planes had failed to do much damage to the German bunkers. "Let's bring

Allied landing craft unload troops and vehicles on D-Day. This photograph from the air captures only part of the huge operation.

Collins over here," shouted Weinberg. He and Joe crawled fifty yards to Collins and dragged him back to the steel shelter. But while the sergeant wrapped a bandage around the stump of Collins's right arm, Collins stopped breathing.

Despite furious enemy fire, American troops moved up the beach toward the cliffs. Joe joined them in a wild dash, firing like a madman. Meanwhile, Sgt. Weinberg crawled away in the opposite direction to pick up a machine gun whose owner had been shot.

Roger, staying where he was, watched Joe in disbelief. The beach was pure chaos. Wounded men were everywhere. Medical officers trying to help the wounded were themselves getting hit. Nearby, American tanks fired wildly at the cliffs. Some were successful, but not all. They were targets, too, and one near Roger caught fire.

Only a few of the soldiers who had landed with Roger were still alive. "Well, I made it this far," thought Roger. "I just have to keep being careful."

Then he saw Joe take a tumble. He sprang into action, running and crawling over to Joe. The cheerful tough guy from the Bronx lay on his back, bleeding from a wound in his stomach. Roger cradled Joe's head in his arm, saying, "You're going to be okay, you're going to make it." Joe, unaware of Roger, cried for his mama. Then he became silent.

Joe's death made Roger's emotions change from fear to anger. "I have a job to do," he thought. Germans in a nearby pillbox kept spraying the beach with machine-gun fire. Roger, forgetting his own safety, ran screaming toward it. He reached in his pack for a hand grenade. Though a bullet struck his right leg, Roger kept going. He tossed the grenade through the opening in the pillbox. The explosion knocked him to the ground. Then the pillbox was quiet.

Roger struggled toward the cliffs, stopping only to fire his rifle. By late morning, the second and third waves of American troops had come ashore. More Allied tanks arrived and heavily damaged the German defense. The tide of battle was turning. Someone dressed the wound on Roger's leg. Others who were wounded were moved to the waiting landing craft. It would soon be Roger's turn.

The tide of battle was turning.

3,000 Americans died on the beaches of Normandy on June 6, 1944. By the end of the day, huge numbers of American men and tons of equipment had come ashore. The Atlantic Wall had crumbled, and the Allies began pushing inland.

In the weeks that followed, the Allies pushed the Germans back. On August 23, they reached the Seine River south of **Paris**. Two days later, French

---

People and Terms to Know

Paris—capital of France. From 1940 until 1944 it was controlled by German forces.

---

and American troops liberated the French capital after four years of German occupation.

On that day, Roger and Sgt. Weinberg were riding in a jeep with the Allies as they entered Paris in triumph. Roger thought back to the events of D-Day on Omaha Beach. He silently saluted Lieutenant Purvis, Joe Salerno, and others like them. By September 11th, the Allies had freed France, Belgium, and Luxembourg from the Nazis. Germany was next.

◀ This stark monument to an American soldier killed on D-Day was left on the beach at Normandy.

QUESTIONS TO CONSIDER

1. What was the purpose of Operation Overlord?

2. Why did the troops in the first wave of the invasion have the toughest job of all?

3. What is your opinion of the success of the D-Day invasion?

4. Why do you think Roger "silently" salutes Lieutenant Purvis and Joe Salerno long after the D-Day battle was over?

Battles of World War II
by Michael J. H. Taylor

Michael J. H. Taylor gives the details of Germany's invasion of Poland, France, and Russia and follows up with a description of the Allied invasion on D-Day. Pictures from all these battles can be found through-out the book.

The Good Fight: How World War II Was Won
by Stephen E. Ambrose

The wonderful photos, maps, and stories in this book capture the major events of the war.

The Journal of Scott Pendleton Collins: A World War II Soldier
by Walter Dean Myers

Some days for Scott Collins, a marine in World War II, are boring, while others are more interesting. He and the other men have been preparing for some big invasion, and he has no idea just what awaits him when the invasion morning comes.

The Atomic Bomb

BY DEE MASTERS

April 20, 1945

Dearest Wife,

We are taking **Okinawa** a small piece at a time, and every piece has a terrible price in American lives. I don't know if this is any harder than all the other islands we've taken in the Pacific. I guess you could say we're getting better at this sort of thing. What we're really getting better at is dying.

This guy told me that the Japanese have a crazy code called *"bushido."* Every soldier is supposed to fight to the death. They believe surrender

---

People and Terms to Know

Okinawa—island near Japan where one of the bloodiest fights of World War II happened. 5,000 marines died in the landings alone.

Soldiers reported in their wartime diaries the endless waiting in war. To pass
the time, they read magazines, played cards, and wrote letters home.

is a disgrace. I just wonder how we can end this war without killing every one of them. Besides, how many Americans will have to die doing that?

Sorry, I'm tired. I can't remember when I actually slept for more than minutes or ate a real meal. I don't know what keeps us going. We all snapped out of it though when we heard that President Roosevelt died on the 12th of April. He brought us through the **Great Depression** and so close to victory. I wish he could have lived to see the end of this war. Tell everyone that I'm still too mean to die.

God, how I hate the this war!

Love,
Your Husband

*   *   *

May 9, 1945

Dearest Husband,

The European war is over! Germany has surrendered. Why can't the war in the Pacific be over and you be here with me? Everyone is celebrating, but

---

People and Terms to Know

Great Depression—period of terrible economic trouble that began in 1929 and lasted up until World War II. At one point one out of every four American workers was unemployed.

it's hard to feel happy when you are in such danger! May 8 was Victory in Europe Day—V–E Day. It seems it should all be over, and you should be coming home to me. I am looking at your picture right now. I wonder how you will have changed. It's been two

The war certainly isn't over.

years since we've seen each other! My love for you has not changed though. Well, maybe a little. I'm sure I love you more now. Isn't that funny?

Your Lovin' Wife

*   *   *

June 5, 1945

Dearest Lovin' Wife,

The war certainly isn't over. Why do the Japanese keep up the needless deaths and suffering on both sides? I hate them. When we heard that **Tokyo** had been firebombed on March 9 and had burned for two days, I wished I had dropped the bombs myself. Yes, I have changed. I feel full of hate

---

People and Terms to Know

Tokyo—Japan's largest city and its capital.

at times, and sometimes I feel completely empty. Both of these feelings keep me going, but it's you that keeps me alive. How long can this last? I'm looking at your picture. It's almost worn out. Can you send another?

Love,
Your Lonely Husband

*　　*　　*

August 15, 1945

Dearest Husband,

Could any day be better than today? Yes, of course—the day you come back to me. When the news came, it was like the start of a giant party. I didn't know whether to laugh or cry, so I did both. Your mother, dad, sister, me—we all just grin at each other, and then out of nowhere we'll cry. The end is like a fairy tale. The **atomic bomb** is like the prince who rescued us.

In his press release announcing the bomb, President Truman said, "The force from which the

---

People and Terms to Know

atomic bomb—type of explosive that kills people not only with its blast, but also with radiation. An atomic bomb has hundreds of times more killing power than a conventional bomb.

sun draws its power has been loosed against those who brought war to the Far East." Doesn't that sound almost like magic? The scientists who built the bomb must be the most popular men in America today. The only problem is, we don't know who they are! Everything was kept so secret.

One atomic bomb destroyed the entire Japanese city of Hiroshima.

On July 26 when our government warned the Japanese to "Quit the war or face total destruction," I just knew it meant that they were concerned about you guys. Our leaders must have known you were going to have to fight across every inch of Japan. I so hoped Japan would quit, and so I cried on July 29 when it rejected our warning. I was so afraid for you. I was volunteering at the **canteen** on August 6 when that beautiful B-29 bomber nicknamed "Enola Gay" and piloted by Colonel Tibbet dropped the bomb. I couldn't believe it at first when they said that one atomic bomb destroyed the entire Japanese city of Hiroshima. Then on August 9 they dropped a second bomb on Nagasaki.

People and Terms to Know

canteen—club where soldiers are entertained.

We all waited and worried every day for five days. Then Emperor **Hirohito** announced the surrender!

When will you be home? I was so glad when they dropped those bombs. I was so afraid you would be killed in the last days of the war. I was so afraid. Now it's over. When will you be home?

Hurry to me—please
Your Waiting Wife

* * *

September 10, 1945

D earest Wife,

Please try to be patient just a little longer. I have been assigned to the **occupation force** and am in Tokyo (or what's left of it). We arrived on September 2 and passed the battleship *Missouri* where the Japanese were signing the official papers

---

People and Terms to Know

Hirohito (HEER·roh·HEE·toh)—(1901–1989) emperor of Japan during World War II and the postwar years.

occupation force—foreign soldiers controlling a country. The American military ran Japan from 1945 to 1952. The aim was to create a democratic government in Japan and help it rebuild after the war.

---

of their surrender. **Douglas MacArthur** is in charge here, but we haven't seen much of him yet. However, I did see him once with his famous pipe in his mouth!

Tell Mom to start thinking about my home-coming dinner. I want all my favorites. But you are my most favorite!

Your Loving Husband

*   *   *

October 3, 1945

Dear Loving Husband,

I guess I knew you couldn't get home so quickly, but I want you to! Your mother plans your homecoming menu every day. It will take you a week to eat it all.

Did you know they named the two atomic bombs that were dropped? The first one was "Little Boy" and the second one was "Fat Man." Your mother said that maybe it would have been better

---

People and Terms to Know

Douglas MacArthur—(1880–1964) American general who lost the Philippines to Japan in World War II, but later retook them. In the 1950s he was the leader of all United Nations forces in the Korean War.

to have only dropped one bomb. But I think it took two to show the Japanese that they couldn't do anything against such power.

Be very careful. Do your job well, and hurry home to all of us.

Your Impatient-Proud-Joyful Wife

* * *

October 25, 1945

D earest Wife,

I have seen Hiroshima where the bomb was dropped. I don't think **President Truman** had any other choice, but I'm glad that I did not have to make that decision. I am certain that many more people, especially Americans, would have died had it not been dropped. But I'm also afraid we'll

---

People and Terms to Know

President Truman—Harry S. Truman (1884–1972), 33rd president of the United States (1945–1953). Truman made the decision to use atomic bombs on Japan.

▲

An Allied war correspondent looks at the destruction in Hiroshima after the atomic bomb was dropped.

be living under the shadow of that now-famous **mushroom cloud** for a long time.

Hiroshima was totally silent. Everything was destroyed. One bomb had done all that. I had no idea how powerful that bomb was until then.

People and Terms to Know

mushroom cloud—cloud produced by an atomic bomb explosion. It resembles a giant mushroom in shape.

Seventy to eighty thousand people were killed or are missing and presumed dead. At least that many were injured.

You cannot understand, I think, unless you have been there. I'm not sure why I'm writing this. The numbers don't tell the story. I just had to tell this to someone. I had to get it off my chest, I guess.

Your Loving Husband

*   *   *

November 15, 1945

Dearest Husband,

As long as you are alive and safe, I don't care what happened to the devilish Japanese! They did such evil, starting with their surprise attack on Pearl Harbor. They killed civilians and tortured prisoners. They even sent their own men on suicide attacks. Perhaps worst of all, they have caused us to be brutal. They are not human.

I love you so and wish I were there to comfort you. Haven't you been through enough? Must you stay there any longer? Please come home as soon as possible. Don't be sad. Please! I couldn't stand it.

Your Loving Wife

*   *   *

November 21, 1945

Dearest Wife,

Thank you for your love. It is a precious gift. This stay in Japan has been very good for me. For the last four years I have hated the Japanese. We all have. We had to. But when I went to Hiroshima, something happened to me.

We sailed up into the canals. Japanese families stood silently watching us. Some of the kids saw we weren't going to kill them, so they slowly came down around us. They were all skin and bones, and obviously hungry. We took out our lunches and tore our sandwiches into pieces and passed everything around.

Hatfield was with me. Later he said: "You learn to hate with a passion in wartime. If you don't kill your enemy, they'll kill you. But sharing those sandwiches with the people who had been my enemy . . . I could almost feel my hate leaving me. It was almost a spiritual experience."

People and Terms to Know

Hatfield—Mark Hatfield (b. 1922), World War II veteran, governor of Oregon from 1958 to 1968 and U.S. senator from Oregon from 1969 to 1997.

I guess he said it for me. I'm okay now.

The war is over, sweet wife. Let's do all we can to put all of this behind us—for everyone.

Oh, yeah, did I say I'm shipping home in one week? Well, I am. Get ready for the greatest new year you've ever had!

Love,
Your On-the-Way-Home Husband

QUESTIONS TO CONSIDER

1. What is your opinion about the code of honor that encouraged the Japanese to fight even after they had no chance to win?

2. What event changed the husband's feelings about the Japanese?

3. Why do you think President Truman decided to drop the atomic bomb?

4. What do you think the husband means when he writes, "I'm afraid we'll be living under the shadow of that mushroom cloud for a long time"?

In 1999, Shizuko Yamasaki published her experience of having lived through the atomic bomb explosion in Hiroshima. This is a paragraph from her story.

Soon after the blast, our hair began to fall out and Atsunori [her son] developed a serious nose-bleeding problem that continued for years to come. We stayed in Hiroshima in that hot summer to wait for the return of my husband. I wanted to make sure that he had a place to come back to. But there was no word from him even after the war was over. So I visited a former military office on Aug. 29 to ask about my husband. There I was informed that he had died of dengue fever in Singapore on March 29. If only they had told us of his death, we could have been spared from the radiation and hardship that followed.

The Cold War

Heading Toward "Heartbreak"

BY WALTER HAZEN

With the 2nd Division, June 25, 1951

Today marks the first anniversary of this "police action." Yeah, that's what I hear they're calling it. It's like the North Koreans were some kind of criminals trying to steal South Korea. And we're the cops chasing them back to their hideout! When the guys on one side are wearing uniforms and shooting at uniformed guys on the other side, then that's a *war* in my opinion. Maybe calling it a "police action" makes the politicians feel good, and makes the public not so scared. But to a soldier in the middle of it, it's practically insulting!

Wow, I didn't mean to start this journal with anger. I want to be able to show it to my kids and grandkids some day. I guess I'm a little angry

American soldiers take cover during the battle for Heartbreak Ridge.

because I remember about seven months ago, when we were told we'd all be home by Christmas. Well, no one counted on the Chinese jumping into this war—oops, I mean "police action".

Anyhow, if what happened at the **United Nations** two days ago means anything, maybe it will all end soon. Captain Newman told us that the Russian ambassador has proposed a **truce**. The captain says that the Soviet Union seems to be afraid that North Korea and China might lose. If that happened, all of Korea would be lost to the **communists**.

*   *   *

*Near **Kaesong**, July 10, 1951*

Truce talks have actually begun at Kaesong! Maybe the fighting will be over! We Americans are

---

People and Terms to Know

United Nations—or U.N., international peacekeeping organization made up of most of the nations of the world. It was founded in 1945, after the end of World War II, to promote world peace, security, and economic development.

truce—temporary peace during wartime.

communists—people who believe the government should control the whole economy in order to share wealth throughout the community. The Soviet Union was the leading communist country until it broke apart in 1991.

Kaesong—town on Korea's west coast. It is situated at the 38th parallel that divides North and South Korea.

keeping our fingers crossed. (I say "Americans" even though there are soldiers from about 15 other countries here helping South Korea. But most of the troops are American.)

* * *

Near the 38th parallel, August 5, 1951

Well, things have bogged down with the peace talks. It seems that neither side is willing to give an inch. It took them several weeks even to agree on what to talk about!

It took them several weeks even to agree on what to talk about!

I understand the general is getting fidgety. Captain Newman says that's because he's afraid we'll lose our "fighting edge" sitting around waiting to see what happens at Kaesong. To put it another way, I think something big is about to happen.

Until then, we'll just stay where we are. The 38th parallel is just a line on the map. There's no body of water here, nothing to tell you why it's such a big deal. But it *is* a big deal because that's the line that separated North and South Korea before

Korea Divided

SOVIET UNION

CHINA

NORTH
KOREA

Sea of
Japan

• Pyongyang

Truce Line, 1953
38th Parallel

Kaesong

• Seoul

Yellow
Sea

SOUTH
KOREA

N
W — E
S

0   150   300 Miles

0   300 Kilometers

the North crossed it last year. You know, it's one of
those lines of latitude that divide the globe up into
different sections. This same 38th parallel runs right
south of Washington, D.C. Captain Newman says
it's not far from places like Cincinnati or San
Francisco either.

*   *   *

Same place, August 10, 1951

During this break in the fighting, we've been doing what soldiers always consider their right: complaining. Phil Eisner and Mark Smith, two of my buddies, probably expressed the views of a lot of **GIs** in our conversations.

"It stinks!" Phil said. "Here we are in a place most of us couldn't have found on map a few months ago. So we now know that Korea is this country that juts out into the sea between China and Japan. What's the big deal! Here we are, and for what? The way I see it, this is a squabble between the Koreans themselves. We've got no business being here."

"Yeah," agreed Mark. "This isn't our fight. Nobody threatened us or outright attacked us like in World War II. This is the first war we've jumped into when nobody was messing with us."

"Well, here's another thing," Phil added. "For the general to say we're sitting around getting soft is a little much. He sees nothing wrong with

---

People and Terms to Know

GIs—abbreviation standing for "general issue" or "government issue." It refers to soldiers of the U.S. Army.

sending us back into the slaughter just to keep our 'fighting edge,' as he calls it. Frankly, I'd like to see him charge up one of these hills with the enemy throwing all sorts of metal down on top of his head. I think he'd change his tune pretty quickly."

"I'm just going to do what I have to do."

Although I agree somewhat with Phil and Mark, I believe that as soldiers, we have a duty to perform. It doesn't matter what we think about this or that.

"Listen, guys," I said. "I don't like being here any more than you. And I can't see how taking all these hills is going to have any effect on the peace talks, like the bigwigs seem to think. I'm going to do what I'm told and fight to keep myself—and you two—from getting killed. I don't know if we're fighting for democracy, or what. I frankly don't care. I'm just going to do what I have to do."

"That's because you *joined* this man's army," Phil spat out. "Mark and I got ourselves drafted. There's a difference."

Well, I don't see a difference, but I didn't press the point.

*   *   *

▲

An American convoy in northeast Korea comes under fire from Chinese forces.

<u>The Punchbowl</u>, *September 9, 1951*

Something big has happened all right. That's why I haven't written in this journal for a while!

It took us three weeks, but we captured a group of hills the reporters are calling "Bloody Ridge." They certainly named that right! We and the **ROKs** suffered about 2,700 casualties, but the North Koreans and Chinese got the worst of it. They may

---

People and Terms to Know

The Punchbowl—dead volcanic crater near the 38th parallel. Overlooking it were hills where some of the bloodiest fights of the Korean War took place.

ROKs—soldiers of the Republic of Korea, or South Korea.

have lost 5,000 men. They've pulled their troops back to another ridge about three miles to the north. Now it looks like we might be attacking them again.

Phil, Mark, and I were lucky in this one. We came through without a scratch.

* * *

Same area, night, September 15, 1951

Early in the morning two days ago, we attacked this second ridge. It's made up of six hills, each named for its height in meters. The hills are 931, 894, 851, 800, 600, and 520. The numbers make everything so organized, don't they? You'd never know what a nightmare it was, or what a mess. There I go again, getting negative. But this time I have a reason.

Once our big guns stopped firing, we started marching. Our goal was Hill 931. But the North Koreans and Chinese saw us coming and opened up with **mortar** and machine-gun fire. It was murder! Their defensive positions at the top of the hills were strong and well-hidden. That explains why

People and Terms to Know

mortar—referring to a short cannon for firing shells high into the air.

our big guns had had little effect. Somehow we managed to fight our way near the top of 931, but we got hit so hard that we had to retreat all the way back down to the bottom.

It was on the way up the hill that Phil got it. A mortar shell exploded almost on top of him. He died instantly. Mark was cut down by machine-gun fire. His chances of pulling through don't look good.

A mortar shell exploded almost on top of him. He died instantly.

As I helped carry Mark down the hill, I cried like a baby because of Phil. Sure, he complained a lot of the time, but so did the other guys. He didn't deserve to die.

* * *

Heartbreak Ridge, September 20, 1951

I found out this morning that Mark died. They say he never came to after getting wounded. I hope that means he didn't feel much pain.

I'm so down I don't know if I can keep on going.

* * *

Same area, September 27, 1951

Yesterday the attack on the ridge was called off. Our regiment, the 23rd, has almost 1,000 dead and wounded men. The whole division has lost more than 1,600 men. I think the plan now is for the Air Force to blast the top of the hills before we give it another try.

Someone started calling this second group of hills "Heartbreak Ridge." Since I just lost my two best friends there, I'd say that's an appropriate name.

*   *   *

Rest area near the 38th parallel, October 15, 1951

The battle for Heartbreak Ridge is finally over. It ended two days ago when a French unit took Hill 850.

The second attack on the ridge began October 4 when our air force fighter bombers hit the enemy hard. The next day, marine fighter planes hit them again.

One by one, we started taking the hills. Hill 520, which is one of the lowest, turned out to be one of the hardest to take. Each **bunker** had to be knocked out separately. More of our guys were hit before a flamethrower flushed the commies from the last of the bunkers.

Captain Newman told me that the 2nd Division had about 3,700 dead and wounded. Almost half of these are from our regiment. But the North Koreans and Chinese

Most of those defending Heartbreak were either killed or wounded.

lost almost 25,000 men. I'm not surprised, since they refused to surrender. Most of those defending Heartbreak were either killed or wounded.

* * *

Yuma, Arizona, January 2, 1954

I've been home for a few months now, trying to forget Korea. But what happened on Heartbreak Ridge haunts me. Some people say that the fight for those hills was the most bitter battle of the war.

How did our taking of those hills affect things in the long run? Did it mean we dealt a crushing

People and Terms to Know

bunker—strongly built shelter, especially one built underground.

blow to our enemies, so that my grandkids will see democracy in North Korea or China?

I'm not certain that it did.

*　　*　　*

To this day, neither China nor North Korea has a democratic government—South Korea does.

QUESTIONS TO CONSIDER

1. Why did the Russians propose a truce in June 1951?

2. What did the general mean when he said his troops might lose their "fighting edge"?

3. Why was Heartbreak Ridge so difficult to capture?

4. In your opinion, what do the attacks on Bloody Ridge and Heartbreak Ridge show about the Korean War?

5. What is your opinion of the narrator's statement, "I believe that as soldiers, we have a duty to perform. It doesn't matter what we think about this or that"?

U.S. Army *versus* McCarthy

BY STEPHEN CURRIE

Milwaukee, Wisconsin
June 1954

" . . . and it's over the fence! A grand slam for Willie Mays, and the Giants take the lead over the Braves, six to four—"

Cal Miller angrily snapped the radio off. Silence filled the living room.

"I'm sorry, darling," his wife Doris said gently. She was sorry for Cal and his **Milwaukee Braves**. But mostly she was sorry that he took baseball so seriously. Half the time he couldn't even bear to

---

People and Terms to Know

Milwaukee Braves—baseball team now called the Atlanta Braves that played in Milwaukee in the 1950s.

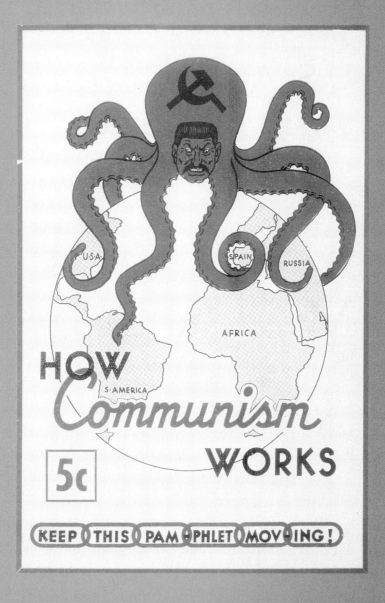

An anti-communist pamphlet shows Soviet leader Joseph Stalin as an octopus whose tentacles represent communist power spreading throughout the world.

listen to the end of a loss. He'd turn the radio off whenever they fell behind.

"Do you mind if I turn on the television?" Doris asked. "The **hearings** are this afternoon."

Cal looked puzzled.

"You know," she added. "They're about **Senator McCarthy** and the army."

"**Tail-Gunner Joe**?" Cal perked up. "Sure, go ahead. He's my kind of guy. Hey, if the Braves lose maybe the senator'll win."

"Maybe," said Doris with less certainty. She turned on the set, found the channel, and adjusted the antenna. Senator McCarthy's face leaped onto the black-and-white screen, his mouth open and his finger raised.

"You tell 'em, Joe," Cal said approvingly.

Doris narrowed her eyes. Oh, she had respect for the senator, all right. She had even voted for him in the last election. And he was raising some very

---

People and Terms to Know

hearings—series of public meetings to determine the truth about a serious situation. In 1954, hearings were held in the Senate about the charges that Senator Joseph McCarthy had made about several Army officials.

Senator McCarthy—(1909–1957) Wisconsin senator Joseph McCarthy, first elected in 1946. Beginning in 1950, he accused many people in the federal government of being traitors with little proof. After hearings in 1954, the Senate punished McCarthy for his actions, and he faded from public view.

Tail-Gunner Joe—nickname given to Senator Joseph McCarthy for the heroics he was supposed to have performed during World War II.

important issues. It was just that something about him was starting to trouble her.

"A *point of order*!" McCarthy crashed his fist on the table in front of him. "A *point of order*!"

Doris started to change the volume control, but the sound was set properly—it was only that the senator was shouting.

"The Army is just like the rest of this country." Cal jabbed his finger at the television set. "It's full of people secretly trying to spread **communism**! First the **Reds** take over the schools and half the government—now they want to take over the Army." He shook his head. "The Russians won't have to fight us. They'll already *own* us."

> "The Russians won't have to fight us. They'll already own us."

"Yes," Doris said slowly. Senator McCarthy had spent four years rooting out communists. These were American men and women who liked the governments of Russia, China, and other enemy

---

People and Terms to Know

point of order—question as to whether the discussion going on in a meeting is allowed by the rules. When someone calls for a point of order, discussion must stop while the chairman decides the question. McCarthy used this rule over and over to interrupt others.

communism—economic and political system based on government ownership of property and businesses and a one-party government.

Reds—nickname for communists.

nations where people weren't free. She remembered the excitement when McCarthy had first told everyone about the traitors in the **State Department**, in the universities, and in the public schools.

"I guess it's good Tom didn't live to see this whole Army business," Cal said softly. His jaw tightened, and his fingers dug into the arm of his chair. "He'd hate to think he gave his life for nothing."

Doris silently stroked her husband's hand. Tom, Cal's younger brother, had been killed three years earlier in the **Korean War**, where he'd gone to fight communism. Doris knew that Cal missed Tom deeply, even after three years. The men had not just been brothers, but best friends.

"Anyone who loves this country ought to oppose the commies," Cal said gruffly as he slid his hand out from under Doris's. "I don't get it. Tom dies to keep us free, and the Reds show up anyway.

People and Terms to Know

State Department—government office in charge of foreign policy.
Korean War—(1950–1953) war in which North Korea and China fought South Korea, which was supported by an international fighting force that was largely American. It was the first war the United States fought against communist countries.

It's a good thing we've got a guy like Senator Joe to stand up for us red-blooded Americans."

Doris nodded. Cal had always been patriotic and he had gotten more so since Tom's death. Doris admired her husband's love for his country. She thought of herself as a patriot, too, but she knew she was not as patriotic as Cal.

There was something odd about McCarthy's patriotism.

Nor was she as patriotic as Senator McCarthy, she thought. But then again, there was something odd about McCarthy's patriotism.

"How did this Army thing start?" Cal asked. "Something about a dentist?"

"That's right," said Doris. The Army lawyer, **Mr. Welch**, came onto the television screen. "A dentist joined the Army," she continued, "and they asked him about his politics, but he wouldn't tell. They were going to discharge him, only then they didn't. The Army said it was an honest mistake—"

"But it wasn't," Cal said. "Senator Joe proved that the general in charge was soft on communism."

People and Terms to Know

Mr. Welch—Joseph Nye Welch, lead lawyer for the Army in the 1954 Senate hearings into Senator McCarthy's charges of communism in the Army.

▲

The Army's chief lawyer, Joseph Welch (seated left), listens to Joseph McCarthy (standing right) during the Army-McCarthy Hearings.

Doris shrugged. She remembered the hearing at which General Zwicker had taken the stand. Perhaps that was when she started to have less confidence in the senator. He had treated the general very rudely. "Anyone with the brains of a five-year-old child could answer that question," he had snapped at Zwicker. McCarthy had not accused the general of being a communist himself, but he had come close to it.

Doris frowned, thinking back. McCarthy had called General Zwicker "A disgrace to the Army." General Zwicker did not know the dentist's political ideas and was only trying to do his job. McCarthy's comment hadn't been very nice. It also hadn't been very—what was the word? She searched her mind, and then she had it.

It hadn't been a very *American* thing to say.

"Well, he *was* soft on communism," Cal said, folding his arms.

Doris glanced toward her husband. She had seen that stubborn, angry look before, when they played checkers and he was about to lose. If he was angry enough, he'd even knock over the board. "That's why they're having the hearings now," she said quietly. "To see who's right, McCarthy or the Army."

Cal snorted. Doris shifted her attention to the television set. McCarthy's face filled the screen, shouting something about a young lawyer named Fisher who worked for Welch. As far as Doris could tell, McCarthy was saying that Fisher belonged to the Lawyer's Guild, a group of lawyers that once was friendly with some communists.

"Go get 'im, Joe!" Cal cried.

Doris wrinkled her nose. It was one thing to be a Red yourself. You couldn't have communists in the United States, making laws and teaching children and running the country. The communists were America's enemies, after all.

But it wasn't fair to be called a Red just because of your friends, or your clubs, or because you'd forgotten to fire a dentist. To McCarthy, she reflected, almost everybody was guilty of being soft on communism.

On the screen, Welch stood up. "May I have your attention, senator?" he asked.

"Ha," said Cal cheerfully. "He's ticked off."

Well, he should be, thought Doris. She felt a little ticked off herself. Young Mr. Fisher had just been called a communist on national television. Most of the people accused by McCarthy had never been found guilty of being communists. Many of them had lost their jobs, though. Many had lost their friends, sometimes even their families.

On the screen, Welch began to talk about Fisher. He said he trusted Fisher, that Fisher had a bright future, and that Fisher was no communist. Doris turned to her husband. "Don't you think the senator should have some proof?" she asked.

"Communists are bad news," Cal said shortly. "Look what they did to Tom."

"Yes," agreed Doris, "but isn't proof important?"

Cal took a deep breath. "They're our enemies," he said. "They killed my brother."

People like Fisher were supposed to be innocent until they were proven guilty.

Doris bit her lip. Communist soldiers *had* killed Tom Miller. That was true. On the other hand, Mr. Fisher hadn't had anything to do with that. At the very worst, he knew people who knew people who actually believed communism might be a good new way of government. Such people were wrong of course. But did they deserve punishment as if they were the North Korean soldiers who had killed Tom? Doris wasn't so sure.

She *was* sure that people like Fisher were supposed to be innocent until they were proven guilty. That was the American way, wasn't it? Senator McCarthy should be trying to defend the American way of life, she thought. It almost seemed that he was attacking it instead. Where was his *proof*?

On the screen, Welch was talking about Fisher. "Little did I dream that you could be so reckless and cruel," he said to McCarthy. "He shall always bear a scar, needlessly inflicted by you."

McCarthy rustled some papers. "I just wanted to give the man's record!" he said loudly. He acted as if it were no big deal, Doris thought, to mention that a man might be an enemy of the United States in front of the whole country.

"You tell 'em, Joe!" Cal said.

Doris sat forward. Something was about to happen. A hush had fallen over the conference room. Earlier, everyone had been looking at the senator. Now, all eyes turned to Welch.

"You've done enough," snapped Welch. "Have you no sense of decency, sir? At long last, have you left no sense of decency?"

McCarthy tried to continue his attack, but Welch did not allow him. "I will not discuss it further," he said. "You, Mr. Chairman, may call the next witness."

There was complete silence in the conference room. And then, one by one, the audience began to clap. People were cheering because Welch had stood up to Senator McCarthy. The applause grew and grew, and after a minute Doris joined in from her seat on the couch.

As for Cal, he snapped off the television set and stormed out of the room.

QUESTIONS TO CONSIDER

1. How would you describe Senator McCarthy?

2. What do you think Cal means when he talks about people being "soft on communism"?

3. What did Welch mean when he said, "He [Fisher] shall always bear a scar, needlessly inflicted by you"?

4. Why does Doris begin to change her mind about McCarthy?

5. Why do you think people agreed with McCarthy at first?

In this part of the Army-McCarthy hearings, the senator insists that he is no more cruel to Fisher than Welch has been to Roy Cohn, one of McCarthy's lawyers. Welch gives the response that helped the American public see how dangerous McCarthy himself was.

SENATOR McCARTHY—May I say that Mr. Welch talks about this being cruel and reckless. He was just baiting—*he* has been baiting Mr. Cohn here for hours, requesting that Mr. Cohn, before sundown, get out of any department of the Government anyone who was serving the communist cause. Now, I just give this man's *record*, and I want to say, Mr. Welch, that it has been labeled [as communist] long before he became a member.

MR. WELCH—Senator, may we not drop this? We *know* he belonged to the Lawyer's Guild.

SENATOR McCARTHY—Let me finish this—

MR. WELCH—And Mr. Cohn nods his head at me. [turning to Roy Cohn] I did you, I think, no personal injury, Mr. Cohn.

MR. COHN—No, sir.

MR. WELCH—I meant to do you no personal injury and if I did, I beg your pardon. [to McCarthy] Let us not assassinate this lad [Fisher] further, Senator. You've done enough. Have you no sense of decency, sir? At long last, have you left no sense of decency?

SENATOR McCARTHY—I know this hurts you, Mr. Welch.

MR. WELCH—I'll say it hurts.

SENATOR McCARTHY—May I say, Mr. Chairman, as a point of personal privilege, that I'd like to finish this.

MR. WELCH—Senator, I think it hurts you too, sir.

The Soviets Launch *Sputnik*

BY JUDITH CONAWAY

$\mathbf{B}$obby spent five years of his childhood in the basement. It started three years before <u>*Sputnik*</u>, in 1954. Bobby was six years old at the time. He spent most of his free time down there because it felt safer.

From hearing his parents talk, Bobby knew that even grownups were afraid. The <u>**Cold War**</u> was starting to heat up. The United States and the <u>**Soviet Union**</u> were competing around the world. A

People and Terms to Know

Sputnik—first manmade object to orbit the earth. It was launched from a rocket by the Soviet Union in 1957.

Cold War—(1945–1991) period of conflict—but rarely all-out war—between the democratic nations of the world, led by the United States, and the communist nations, led by the Soviet Union.

Soviet Union—short for "Union of Soviet Socialist Republics." This was an empire made up of Russia and nearby nations it controlled. The Soviet Union was formed in 1917 and broke apart in 1991.

Kidde
Kokoon

CANNED WATER

Cold War tensions prompted some American families to build bomb shelters.

lot of people thought it was only a matter of time before the competition turned into outright war.

In the "space race," each side was blasting rockets farther and farther away from Earth. In the "arms race," each side was building more and more powerful **nuclear weapons**. A lot of Americans, like Bobby's parents, were preparing for nuclear war. That's why they didn't mind that Bobby spent so much time in the basement. His playroom down there was also a **fallout shelter** that the whole family would stay in if nuclear weapons exploded anywhere near them.

Bobby didn't understand nuclear war, or the Cold War either. But he did know that his enemies were communists. Of course, Bobby had no clear idea of what communism was. But he knew where communists lived. His father showed him. Most

---

People and Terms to Know

nuclear weapons—weapons powered by splitting atoms, the smallest building blocks of matter. When this happens, huge amounts of energy are released, and entire cities can be wiped out by one bomb.

fallout shelter—underground place built to protect people from the effects of nuclear bombs. Fallout is the name for tiny, often radioactive, pieces of material that fall from the sky, often well after a blast of such a bomb. They can cause serious illness or death.

were on the opposite side of the globe from the United States, in China and Russia.

Russia was another name for the Soviet Union, or U.S.S.R. Bobby could see on the globe how huge this country was. China was pretty big too. Together, Russia and China were much bigger than the United States.

Together, Russia and China were much bigger than the United States.

"Don't worry, Bobby," his dad said. "They're bigger, but we're better."

During 1955, the "space race" got much faster. Both the United States and the Soviet Union had plans to launch **satellites** into orbit. Their goal was to do this by 1957.

Bobby didn't pay too much attention to space. He was interested in model airplanes instead. He spent hours down in his playroom, assembling American and Russian fighter jets. His dad worked with him sometimes, showing him what to do.

People and Terms to Know

satellites—objects that orbit around a larger body in space. These objects can be man-made or natural, like a moon.

In 1956, Bobby turned eight. During that year, the United States and the Soviet Union came close to war in several "hot spots" around the world.

Americans were especially worried about the Soviet threat to Europe. The nations of Eastern Europe were called Soviet "satellites." In late 1956, the Soviet army put down revolts in Poland and Hungary, two eastern European nations.

Khrushchev, the Soviet Union's leader, bragged about this victory for communism. "History is on our side," he said to the United States and the other democratic nations. "We will bury you!"

Bobby's dad explained to him why the Soviets were our enemies. The Soviet Union was a **dictatorship**. In the Soviet Union, the Communist Party government owned almost everything and controlled every part of people's lives. Anyone who spoke or wrote against the government got sent to prison or killed.

From movies and comic books, Bobby learned that the communists were trying to take over the

---

People and Terms to Know

Khrushchev (kroosh•CHOF)—Nikita Khruschev (1894–1971), leader of the Soviet Union from 1953 to 1964 during the height of the Cold War.

dictatorship—absolute rule of a country by one strong central power, with no guarantees for the rights of the citizens.

whole world. They were getting stronger and coming closer. In fact, there were many secret communists living in ordinary neighborhoods, spying for the Soviet Union.

One day one of Bobby's neighbors asked if he could see Bobby's model airplanes. Bobby said yes, but he was secretly worried. What if the neighbor was a spy, trying to find out what kind of planes the Americans had?

Bobby soon figured out that this was a silly thing to worry about. The neighbor had a grown-up son who was pilot in the U.S. Air Force.

But Bobby kept being worried about Soviet bombs. At school, his class started practicing for enemy attacks. When an alarm went off, the students would huddle under their desks for protection. Sometimes they would go out in the hallway and crouch along the wall.

The year 1957 began with a proud event for all Americans. On January 18, three jet planes from the United States Air Force flew nonstop around the world. At school, Bobby learned how to make a "jet" airplane with a balloon. First he taped a balloon to a paper airplane. He blew up the balloon.

Then he let it go and watched the air move the plane forward.

After school, in his basement playroom, Bobby tried the same experiment with one of his models. The jet fighter crashed against his family's washing machine. It took him an hour to repair his model.

On October 4, 1957, the Soviet Union launched **Sputnik,** *the first satellite to orbit the earth.*

In September 1957, Bobby entered the fourth grade. He was nine now and really looking forward to the start of school. He had a huge collection of model planes to show off, and even a few model rockets. In the last week of September he had his own day of "show and tell." He showed off all his model planes and rockets.

But Bobby did not enjoy his feelings of pride for long. On October 4, 1957, the Soviet Union launched *Sputnik*, the first satellite to orbit the earth. Americans were stunned and scared by this Soviet success. It was clear that the Soviets had pulled ahead in the "space race." Were they pulling ahead in the "arms race" too?

Bobby was crushed, of course. Suddenly his model planes looked just like toys.

▲

The Soviet Union's launching of the *Sputnik* satellite was a major event.

On November 3, 1957, the Soviets launched a second satellite, *Sputnik II*. This satellite carried a dog named Laika—the first living creature to be blasted into space. On November 10, *Sputnik II* stopped sending signals back to Earth. The satellite did not end its orbit until April 13, 1958.

Bobby cried when he thought about poor Laika, dying alone out there in space. He just couldn't help himself. After he stopped crying, he got really angry. His father had told him that the Soviets were evil. Now he knew it was true.

On January 31, 1958, the United States finally launched its own satellite, *Explorer I*. This satellite was a huge success. It carried equipment that made an important scientific discovery—the **Van Allen radiation belt**.

Americans started to feel proud again. "It took us a bit longer," said Bobby's dad, "but we did it a lot better."

After *Explorer I*, Bobby still spent a lot of time in the basement. But he stopped building model airplanes and started building model spacecraft. He also started reading science fiction stories about outer space. He daydreamed about becoming a scientist and helping beat the communists once and for all.

Gradually, Bobby was starting to come up from underground. He got a paper route to help pay for his growing collection of space toys and comic books. After dinner, he stayed upstairs to watch the evening news with his parents. Now he could better understand what was going on in the world.

At school, Bobby's teachers paid much more attention to math and science. Bobby had always

---

People and Terms to Know

Van Allen radiation belt—area of high magnetism that surrounds Earth. It was discovered by American scientist James A. Van Allen.

done well in science, so now he became one of the stars of his class. He spent more time with his friends.

Whenever the United States or the Soviet Union launched a satellite, Bobby and his friends would go outside late at night. They would look up the sky, searching for a tiny dot that seemed to be gliding through the stars.

For Bobby's eleventh birthday, in 1959, his parents gave him a telescope. After that he hardly ever went down into the basement at all.

QUESTIONS TO CONSIDER

1. What was *Sputnik?*

2. How did the United States and the Soviet Union compete against each other during the Cold War?

3. What actions by the Soviet Union made people in the United States afraid?

4. How did people in the United States react to *Sputnik I* and *Sputnik II?*

5. What was the first United States satellite to orbit the earth, and what did it discover?

6. How do you think the launching of *Sputnik* affected American education?

Friendship 7: First American in Orbit
by Michael D. Cole

Manned spaceflight came soon after Sputnik, and Michael D. Cole's book describes just what it was like to be one of the first astronauts. Space travel was dangerous in the beginning, and astronauts had to face difficult training long before their missions started.

The History News: In Space
by Michael Johnstone

Can you imagine what it was like to see rockets and astronauts on the front page of the newspaper for the first time? This book has made history into headlines on space discoveries from the time the ancient peoples first started looking at the stars.

The U.S. Space Camp Book of Rockets
by Anne Baird and Buzz Aldrin

Sputnik, the first satellites, and the first astronauts were carried into space on rockets. In this book you can follow a group of Space Camp students on a tour of the rocket park in Huntsville, Alabama. Not only will you see the rockets that took astronauts to the moon, but you will also get a chance to look at a space station of the future.

Cuban Missile Crisis

BY DANNY MILLER

*K**ennedy** to Speak to Nation Tonight!* On October 22, 1962, the headline of the *Chicago Tribune* was larger than usual. As he did every morning, Max Rosen stacked the newspapers on the shelves of his newsstand. The bold headline seemed to catch the attention of everyone who walked by. So President Kennedy was going to discuss a matter of "national importance." Max wondered what that could be.

"I'll bet it has something to do with **Cuba**," said Mr. Larson, one of Max's regular customers. "My brother works in the State Department in

---

People and Terms to Know

Kennedy—John Fitzgerald Kennedy (1917–1963), 35th president of the United States (1961–1963); assassinated in November 1963, the year after the Cuban Missile Crisis.

Cuba—small island country in the Caribbean Sea, off the southern coast of Florida.

President Kennedy told the American people on October 22, 1962, that the
United States was setting up a naval blockade against Cuba.

Washington, D.C., and he told me there's some kind of situation down there. That island has never been the same since **Fidel Castro** took over in 1959."

"I know," agreed Max. "Since he turned Cuba into a communist country, the Soviet Union has a friend only 90 miles from Florida! That is way too close for comfort!"

According to the newspaper, the speech would be broadcast on television!

"Well, we'll know tonight!" Mr. Larson said as he left. Max liked talking with him, but he wasn't sure that his brother should be sharing government secrets with him. But Max supposed it couldn't really hurt—in a few hours the subject of Kennedy's talk wouldn't be a secret any more. According to the newspaper, the speech would be broadcast on television!

B y the time he got home that evening, Max was very eager to have his family hear the president. Amanda Rosen, his wife, stopped stirring the beef

---

People and Terms to Know

Fidel Castro—born in 1926, political leader of Cuba since 1959. The revolution he led that year made Cuba the first communist state in the same part of the world as the United States.

stew that was for dinner. She was a big fan of President Kennedy. She took off her apron and joined her husband in the living room.

There Max was warming up the large television set. It took a while for the black-and-white picture to appear on the screen. There was even enough time for Amanda to call the Rosen children and have them take their places around the set.

Fifteen-year-old Billy sat down next to his father. Billy liked to keep track of world events. He even thought he might go into politics one day. Eleven-year-old Julia sat on the floor with her sixth-grade science book. Julia wanted to be an astronaut and hoped women would be allowed to go into space soon. Who knows—some day people might even land on the moon! She knew Kennedy helped the space program. Maybe that was the subject of his talk tonight.

"Look," said Amanda Rosen, taking her place on the sofa. "It's about to start!" The whole family stared at the flickering image of President John F. Kennedy sitting behind his desk in the **Oval Office**.

People and Terms to Know

Oval Office—president's office in the White House, the Presidential home in Washington, D.C.

"Good evening, my fellow citizens," Kennedy began. He sounded very serious. Mr. and Mrs. Rosen leaned closer to the set. The president explained that our government had been watching the Soviet military buildup in Cuba. So Mr. Larson had been right!

Within the past week, American planes over the island took pictures that proved that the Soviets had been building missile sites in Cuba. These sites would allow them to launch missiles that could reach most U.S. cities in a matter of minutes!

Cuban Missile Crisis

Billy got angry with the Soviet leader. "That sneaky Khrushchev!" he said. "He thought he could pull a fast one on America, but we caught him!"

"Shhh!" said Julia sharply. She wanted to hear what the United States was going to do now.

Kennedy explained that he was ordering a **blockade** of all arms being sent to Cuba by ship. He said that if any missiles were launched from Cuba, the United States would launch a full attack on the Soviet Union. He called on Khrushchev to end what he called a "reckless" threat to world peace. "We have no wish to war with the Soviet Union."

The Rosens sat frozen in place, even as the president left the screen and the reporters began talking. Max turned off the TV without saying anything. When Julia finally broke the silence, she sounded a little scared. "Mom, Dad, what does it mean? Are we going to war with Russia?"

"I certainly hope not," said Max. "But Kennedy was right to order the blockade. The Soviets broke their promise not to build missile bases in Cuba. We have to do something."

People and Terms to Know

blockade—use of ships or troops to prevent movement into and out of a port or region controlled by an enemy.

Mrs. Rosen was worried. During World War II she had lost two uncles in the fighting, and many of her relatives living in Europe were also killed. Now suddenly there could be a deadly war right here in America!

The nuclear-powered aircraft carrier *Enterprise* was one of the U.S. warships blockading Cuba.

Later that evening, the local news carried Khrushchev's response to Kennedy's speech. He claimed that the blockade was unfair. He would not stop the ships already on their way to Cuba.

Over the next few days, American flags popped up all over the Rosens' neighborhood. These were signs of support for Kennedy's actions.

In his store Max couldn't keep the newspapers on the stands. Everyone wanted to know the latest about what was happening. When the newspapers sold out, people started asking *him* questions about the crisis. It was as if they thought he was a reporter just because he sold newspapers! Mr. Rosen did his best to answer their questions, but he knew little more than they did. He decided to ask Mr. Larson if he had any more news from his brother in Washington.

We are in as serious a crisis as mankind has been in.

Mr. Larson did. He told Max that after Kennedy's speech, the secretary of state had said that we are in as serious a crisis as mankind has been in. Leaders of other countries were also starting to get nervous. Everyone seemed to think that the world was heading toward a war. Max thanked

Mr. Larson, but that wasn't the kind of news he was going to like telling his neighbors. People were worried enough as it was.

At Julia's school there was an **air-raid drill**. "Duck and cover," chanted her teacher. The children crouched next to their lockers and put their hands over their heads. Julia wondered if this would really protect them if the Russians dropped a bomb on Chicago. She was pretty sure it wouldn't.

All of Billy's teachers talked about the crisis. In geography class Mrs. O'Connor showed how close the missile sites were to the United States. Mr. Andrews, the history teacher, talked about the troubles between the Soviet Union and the United States.

Although the two countries had fought on the same side in World War II, things had gotten worse since the war ended. America was very much against the Soviet Union's trying to spread communism to other countries. For years both countries had been spending huge amounts of money to develop deadly weapons in case the other one attacked.

People and Terms to Know

air-raid drill—practice exercise to prepare for an attack by planes dropping bombs.

On Saturday morning, the Rosens went to their temple to pray for peace. Panic was in the air and people openly talked about the possibility of World War III. Some neighbors were even building bomb shelters in their backyards and buying lots of canned food in case there was a war. Mrs. Rosen called her parents in New York and tried not to cry. Would she ever see them again?

Back at his store, Max sold triple the number of newspapers that he usually sold on a Saturday. For once he was not happy about the extra business.

Mr. Larson ran in with news that an American spy plane had just been shot down over Cuba. Max thought this was very bad news. Was there about to be an all-out war that would kill millions of Americans? He decided to close the store early and head home to be with his family.

That night, the Rosens tried to forget their worries. They went to a theater downtown to see a movie called *West Side Story* that had been playing for a long time. It was a musical update of the play *Romeo and Juliet* set in present-day New York. The clash between the two gangs in the movie reminded Billy of what was going on between the

United States and the Soviet Union. No matter what the characters did in the movie, there seemed to be no way to avoid violence and death.

Kennedy had received an important message from Khrushchev.

On Sunday morning, October 28, Max Rosen was almost afraid to look at the newspapers that were bundled up when he arrived at his newsstand. President Kennedy hadn't been seen in days. Max read that he was in constant meetings with his closest advisors, including his brother, Attorney General **Robert F. Kennedy.**

When the telephone rang, Max nearly jumped out of his skin! It was his wife. Amanda had just heard on the radio that Kennedy had received an important message from Khrushchev. Max quickly closed the newsstand and ran all the way home to hear what the Soviet leader had said. Would it be war or peace?

People and Terms to Know

Robert F. Kennedy—(1925–1968) brother of President John F. Kennedy and U.S. attorney general (1961–1964) who led a major fight against organized crime. Later a senator from New York (1965–1968), Robert Kennedy was assassinated in 1968 as he ran for president.

The entire Rosen family huddled around the television set watching the reports of Khrushchev's amazing words.

"The Soviet government . . . has given a new order to dismantle the arms which you describe as **offensive**, and to crate them and return them to the Soviet Union."

President Kennedy's response quickly followed. He welcomed the Soviet decision, calling it an important "contribution to peace." For his part, Kennedy promised that the U.S. would not invade Cuba in the future. The crisis seemed to be over!

Mr. and Mrs. Rosen hugged their children tightly. Billy went upstairs to write a letter to President Kennedy. Billy said that he was the best president ever and that he would surely be reelected in 1964. Julia ran to her bedroom in relief and started playing **Elvis Presley**'s newest hit, "Return to Sender."

She thought it would be funny to play this song for the ships taking the missiles back to the Soviet Union.

People and Terms to Know

offensive—for the purpose of attacking rather than defending.
Elvis Presley—(1935–1977) major music and movie star in the 1950s and 1960s. To this day, Presley is called the "King" of rock 'n roll.

QUESTIONS TO CONSIDER

1. What was the matter of "national importance" that President Kennedy spoke to the nation about on October 22, 1962?

2. Why was the United States worried that the Soviet Union was building missile sites in Cuba?

3. What was the mood of the American people during the crisis?

4. Why were some Americans building bomb shelters and storing up food?

5. How was the Cuban missile crisis finally resolved?

6. What do you think about the way President Kennedy handled the crisis?

The Vietnam Era

Jungle Warfare

BY BRIAN J. MAHONEY

Many a time I sat in a helicopter floating over the oceans of green jungle below. Sometimes you could swear you were in heaven. If the other guys kept quiet, you might drift off and think big thoughts like, "Why are we here, anyway?" By "here" I mean **Vietnam**. And though we didn't talk about it much, I know I wasn't the only fighting man who wondered what I was doing there. Politicians gave speeches about how America had to stop the spread of communism. But to me, this didn't always make sense. Vietnam's a small country, not like Russia or China. I don't see how it could ever

People and Terms to Know

Vietnam—country in Southeast Asia. In 1954 it was divided into two countries, North and South Vietnam. Beginning in the 1960s, U.S. forces fought to protect South Vietnam from control by the North. See the map on page 26.

hurt us if we just stayed home and minded our own business. This was someone else's **civil war**.

My dad was the one who said I ought to sign up for the military. "Sure, I'll go and fight," I said. "You survived a bigger war than this one. Vietnam should be a piece of cake."

In Vietnam it was hard to tell the enemy from the guy who served you lunch.

I said the words that made Dad smile, but inside I wasn't so confident. He fought in France against German tanks that were right out where you could see them. And if he helped kick the enemy out of a small French town, the people treated him like a hero. Dad was full of stories like that.

The **Vietnam War** was different from World War II. We sometimes dealt with villages who wanted the "bad guys" to win. Maybe they even thought *we* were the bad guys—after all, we were the ones pretty much invading their land. So you were

---

People and Terms to Know

civil war—war fought within a single country by its own people.

Vietnam War—(1955–1975) war between communist North Vietnam and South Vietnam. South Vietnam was supported by U.S. troops from 1965 until 1973 and surrendered in 1975.

always on your toes. In Vietnam it was hard to tell the enemy from the guy who served you lunch.

Life was day by day in 'Nam. I learned not to think about things like home, pretty women, TV shows, and steak dinners. You best think about **Charlie** hiding behind the next bush with an **AK-47** leveled at your chest. You're in his backyard. If you let your mind wander too much, your soul will soon be joining it. Of course you could die even if you were paying attention and doing your job. That's what happened to Mikey. That's what happened to Tyrone when he got blown up in my **foxhole**.

We lost them on one of those days when we knew something was going to happen. Our chopper dropped from the sky and headed for the smoke that was used to mark the landing zone. I was just a month shy of ending my first **tour of duty**.

They dropped us in a place a few miles north of our base camp. It looked like any other place I'd been to, except this place had a lot of body bags piled to greet us. The chopper brought us in, and then it was loaded up with the unlucky guys that

---

People and Terms to Know

Charlie—nickname for the United States' enemy in the Vietnam War.
AK-47—rifle used by communist forces in Vietnam.
foxhole—hole dug for protection in combat.
tour of duty—period of military service during war time.

got it from Charlie last night. The survivors, or "live bodies" as we called them, didn't say what happened. Their eyes said more than their mouths did. But I didn't really need to know the details anyway. If it's your time, it's your time.

Anyway, on this particular night Sarge wanted Tyrone and Mikey up toward the front of the group. Tyrone was a black, hard-as-nails coal miner's son. He could spot a **land mine** on a moonless night at a full run. If you wanted to make it out of there alive, you'd stick with Tyrone.

Mikey was different. He never got rid of that "new meat" smell, you know what I mean? He was just like a little kid inside, but he'd take a .45 pistol and flashlight and crawl into a booby-trapped **Vietcong** tunnel complex all alone. He'd come out smiling hundreds of feet away and tell us what he'd seen. Charlie had underground rooms with beds, a hospital, and all the comforts of home! I guess I liked

---

People and Terms to Know

land mine—small bomb or similar device buried in the ground and set to explode when stepped on or run over by a vehicle. Land mines left over from earlier wars are responsible for thousands of deaths and injuries each year worldwide.

Vietcong (vee•eht•KAHNG)—South Vietnamese Communists who, with North Vietnamese support, fought against the government of South Vietnam in the Vietnam War.

these two guys because they were like the two sides of me—half soldier, half goofy kid.

Anyway, our plan was to march into the jungle and wait to **ambush** the enemy. Then later, Charlie might think twice about moving through there. But it wasn't going to be a permanent victory. That's 'cause the ground here changes hands more than a pretty girl at a dance full of lonely soldiers. The difference is that at this dance, people die.

We cut our way through the bush with machetes, through the snakes, up the hills, down the hills.

We cut our way through the bush with **machetes**, through the snakes, up the hills, down the hills. We made our own trail. If you take an old trail, you might find yourself shot, or missing a leg from a mine. Or, worse yet, you land in a trap with stakes. That's right, the enemy puts sharpened sticks face-up at the bottom of a hidden hole. One bad step and they go through your boot and your

---

People and Terms to Know

ambush—planned surprise attack on moving enemy troops.
machetes (muh·SHEHT·eez)—long knives used for cutting vegetation.

foot. And wounds don't heal too well out here—it's too wet, hot, and sticky. Sometimes insects will get in them too.

We marched to a spot near where the other Americans had been killed last night. Sarge thought Charlie might be poking around again, so we set up the mines and rigged them to a hand switch that our guy on watch could trip when Charlie got close.

Tyrone and I dug a hole and got our gear ready. Before I caught some zzzz's, Tyrone told me (again!) about his hometown and his mama's lemonade. "Back home, nights like this, we'd just sit by the river and talk about whatever," he said, laughing. "Ahhh, drinkin' that lemonade, watchin' my nieces play, and just talkin'—no killin' or listenin' to crazy folks talkin' nonsense."

"That's funny, Tyrone," I said, "I think you're kind of crazy, and you never make much sense."

"Hey, I know it, but I still got more sense than you!" he winked. "You just wait 'till we get outta here and you come down and have a sip of mama's lemonade!"

"I will, my brother! Hey, where's Mikey?" I asked.

Tyrone looked up at the night sky, "I don't know—Sarge sent him up there to watch . . . "

BOOM! Ratta-tatta BOOM!

Charlie must've crept up and tripped a mine because suddenly the jungle was alive with rifle flashes. I got out my weapon and aimed at the flashes. Tyrone ducked and threw grenades at the clusters of light.

Somehow Charlie got through, because he was among us in no time. Three Vietcong soldiers fell on Tyrone first. He threw one away, so I took him out when he landed. Tyrone finished the others with the knife he took from the first guy who jumped him. Grenades started coming through and pinned us down in the hole.

Then something hit my leg. I looked just in time to see Tyrone hit the deck and get blown up from underneath. I was shocked dumb. Did he just fall on a hand grenade for me? Is that what just happened? I couldn't get it through my head. Tyrone was my hero—unstoppable. I turned him over, and he smiled at me and died at the bottom of our hole. Later we found what was left of Mikey. He was supposed to be the key guy in our ambush—our trap for the Vietcong, but it turned out he was the one who got ambushed.

That's it. I don't have any moral to tell you. There's no point in good men dying, even if you call them heroes later on.

▲

A U.S. paratrooper guides a helicopter into a gap in the jungle to pick up the wounded and dead.

When my tour ended, I went right to the <u>VA hospital</u> where my dad had been laid up for two months. When the nurse let me into his room, he

People and Terms to Know

VA hospital—hospital run by the Veterans Administration.

was sleeping. His breath made noises that weren't good, and I wondered how much time he had left.

When he woke up and saw me, though, his face lit up with happiness. "Well, now you're a veteran, son," he said. "How does that feel?"

Didn't he know that with this war, there were protest marches instead of parades?

"Uh, I guess it feels good, Dad." I didn't know how to answer his question in any simple way.

"When you're a veteran," he went on, "you get treated differently. Take this hospital, for instance. I get free medical care whenever I need it. And holidays like Memorial Day and Veterans Day will mean more to you. Hey, you won't be watching the parades from the side any more—you'll be in them!"

"I can hardly wait, Dad," I said. Then I changed the subject. I wondered if Dad watched TV at all. Didn't he know that with this war, there were protest marches instead of parades? Didn't he know that people called us killers more often then they called us heroes?

A couple of weeks later I took a bus across three states so I could visit Tyrone's grave in his hometown. Seeing his name like that on the tombstone did something to me. I heard him calling out to me like he used to when he realized we had both lived through a fight. I imagined him inviting me to have that cool drink of lemonade he was always bragging about.

When I thought about how he never got that glass of lemonade, I lost my strength and wanted to cry. But I couldn't. I was too angry to cry, and that made me even angrier. I started shouting, and I'm sure the folks who were there putting flowers on granny's grave thought I was some kind of crazy man. I kept shouting the same question over and over again.

Where's *our* parade, Dad?

I'm still waiting.

QUESTIONS TO CONSIDER

1. How was fighting in Vietnam different from fighting in World War II?

2. What were some of the dangers of being a soldier in the Vietnam War?

3. According to the narrator, what were the causes of the Vietnam War?

4. What did the narrator admire about Tyrone and Mikey?

5. What is your opinion of the way U.S. soldiers in Vietnam were received when they came home?

Sing for Your Father, Su Phan
by Stella Pevsner and Fay Tang

Su Phan does not pay much attention to the war—until Communist soldiers come to her village. They take her father to prison and make her village a war zone. Su Phan and her family must flee, and the journey will be dangerous.

A Place Called Heartbreak: A Story of Vietnam
by Walter Dean Myers

This is a true story about Major Fred V. Cherry, an African-American pilot during the Vietnam War. In 1965 his plane was shot down, and he was captured in North Vietnam. He was a prisoner of war for seven years. Walter Dean Myers describes how Major Cherry survived those difficult years.

The Valiant Women of the Vietnam War
by Karen Zeinert

Karen Zeinert describes how women's roles changed with the Vietnam War. More women became doctors, volunteers, members of the media, and joined the armed forces. Zeinert includes special sections on Major General Jeanner Holm, the first female general in the U.S. Air Force, and Mary Beth Tinker, a young protest leader.

Black Soldiers in Vietnam

BY JUDITH LLOYD YERO

I was the first person in my family to finish high school. This was 1963. I couldn't go to college because my folks couldn't afford it. I'm 17 years old and I don't have any job skills—who's gonna hire me? So the only thing left was to go into the service. I didn't want the Army. The Navy I didn't like because of the uniforms. But the Marines were *bad*—they built men. Plus, they had all those John Wayne movies on every night, showing how the Marines got the job done.

At first, **boot camp** wasn't like I expected. These were the Marines—these were the good guys. So

---

People and Terms to Know

boot camp—camp where people who have just joined the military go for basic training.

An African-American soldier keeps watch in the Vietnamese jungle.

why were they callin' me all kinds of names? There was a lot of racial stuff and that blew my mind.

After a while, things got better. I guess sometimes it takes a tragedy, like a hurricane or a flood—or a war—to bring people together. In boot camp, a lot of the guys found themselves living with people of different racial backgrounds for the first time in their lives. Suddenly you say, hey, some of these people are brighter than you are or as bright as you are. You realize they're stronger than you, or that they're just as capable as you are, yet they're part of a different race. These are things that you might not think about back home, where the races are separated so much. At boot camp we were all thrown together.

> *A lot of the guys found themselves living with people of different racial backgrounds for the first time in their lives.*

Once we were in 'Nam, I saw how easy it was for anyone to fall into the racist thing—even me. We didn't know anything about the enemy. In boot camp, we were told that the **VC** were the bad guys. We were told that they took rice from villagers and

---

People and Terms to Know

VC—short for the Vietcong, South Vietnam Communists who fought for North Vietnam.

killed American soldiers. Nobody told us about their history or their values—they were just the enemy. And we were Americans—even if a lot of people back home didn't treat us that way. So it was easy to start thinking, "We're the heroes from the powerful U.S.A. and they're just animals who live in the jungle." The actual truth was that the war turned *all* of us into animals.

In 'Nam, the enemy never called us the names we heard back home, but we still didn't call them "Vietnamese." Sometimes we called them "Victor Charlie," the code for VC. A lot of times we just shortened that down to "Charlie." But we also called the Vietnamese other names that were just as bad as what we heard at home. Whether you were black, Hispanic, white, Indian, or whatever, if you were an American in Vietnam, you called the VC really bad names. I guess everyone got to see and feel the most ugly side of racial and ethnic hatred.

My black friends in the Marines never had white friends at home, so we pretty much hung together at first. And I guess it was the same for the white guys. They'd never really known a black guy. Pretty soon, we figured out that when things got tough—when we were out where the shooting was—we all wanted the same thing. We wanted to get out of there alive. If you didn't hang together, Charlie would wipe out the whole **platoon.** So it didn't matter what color your skin was or where you came from—you stuck together.

Even Reverend King had taken to speaking out against the war.

There were new guys comin' in from the States all the time—from Detroit, Chicago, from Tupelo, Mississippi, and other places. They would tell us what was goin' on back home. A lot of blacks there said we had no business fightin' the white man's war—that there were plenty of battles to fight at home. **Ali** refused to serve. He said no Vietnamese had ever treated him the way white people did— never called him names—so he had no argument with them.

Even **Reverend King** had taken to speaking out against the war. What he said made sense to a lot of

---

People and Terms to Know

platoon—military group of about 45 soldiers commanded by a lieutenant.

Ali—Muhammad Ali, famous African-American heavyweight boxer who refused to be drafted into the military during the Vietnam War.

Reverend King—Dr. Martin Luther King, Jr. (1929–1968), minister who led the African-American civil rights movement in the United States from the mid-1950s until his assassination in 1968.

▲

African-American soldiers in Vietnam sit and eat together.

us. He said it was strange to send young black men 8,000 miles away to protect the rights of people in Vietnam. You see, these blacks didn't enjoy a lot of those same rights in certain places in *America*. King pointed out that boys of different colors were dying together though back home they couldn't go to the same schools.

Sometimes the brothers would get together and talk about the problems. We would talk about what we would do when we got home. There was the question about whether we should keep doin' our duty or revolt.

It didn't help that **Hanoi** was sending the same message over the radio. Nothing would have made the enemy happier than if black soldiers started puttin' down the war. It was the blacks who volunteered for the toughest jobs—who made up the elite groups of the military—the special forces and airborne riflemen. Hanoi was telling us stuff like when two black guys killed in 'Nam went home, some whites wouldn't let them be buried in their cemeteries.

We weren't stupid. We knew that white guys could often afford to go college, and we couldn't. See early in the war, if you were in college, you could get out of serving in the military. Or if your family had enough money, they could send you to some faraway country and you could avoid the war. So who do you think was left to fight? I'll tell you who—it was the poor and the badly educated Americans. That meant many blacks had to serve. But at least here we had a chance to show what we could do. We got some respect. When we did our

People and Terms to Know

Hanoi—capital of North Vietnam, where the leaders of its government and military were based.

jobs or saved someone from getting shot, we felt good about it.

We had pride. When you saw a brother, you did the **dap**. The whole idea of saying "I'm black and I'm proud"—people back then never heard anything like that. And all of a sudden, it became something important to us black soldiers who may have come from very poor families. Some of the white guys didn't get that we were just showing we were proud to be black. They thought it was some kind of threat. But that didn't change the way we felt.

It didn't matter what color your skin was when the shooting started. You had to work together if you wanted to live. But maybe the people against the war were right. If we couldn't even get a job when we got home, what's the point? Then I think, even though heroes in the movies are always white, that doesn't mean black soldiers haven't fought with honor in all the other American wars. And I guess we're not going to change that now.

One day I saw 12 men die. Two were from Puerto Rico, one was Jewish, and one was black.

People and Terms to Know

dap—complicated way of shaking hands or greeting one another. It was started by African-American troops.

The others were white men whose families had come to America from Europe. But the only color I saw was red—the color of the blood of 19-year-old kids who had been the victims of a terrible tragedy.

QUESTIONS TO CONSIDER

1. Why did the narrator expect to be treated differently once he joined the Marines?

2. What kinds of lessons did young men of all races learn when they joined the military?

3. Why were poor Americans more likely to fight in Vietnam than wealthy Americans?

4. Why did the black soldiers have mixed feelings about fighting in Vietnam?

5. Why do you think that Reverend King's argument against the war included the point that many African-American children still didn't go to white schools?

A "Living Room War"

BY JUDITH CONAWAY

Hector Martinez, Jr., came home from the Vietnam War in February 1967. His family was waiting when Hector was carried off the plane. They were all shocked when they saw him. He was in a body cast. It was a stiff covering made of a kind of plaster. Its purpose was to hold his bones and muscles in place.

"Hey, don't look at me like that," said Hector, with his familiar grin. "I'm still in here, man."

Hector's mother kissed him. His father cried. His sisters, cousins, uncles, and aunts crowded closer. "I'll be out of this mummy case in no time," joked Hector. "They wrapped me up extra just for the trip."

An American couple watches coverage of the Vietnam War on their television.

Fortunately, Hector was right. At the hospital, they cut him loose and put his arms and legs in separate casts. Soon he was sitting up in bed looking much more like his old self.

But he wasn't really the same old Hector. Everyone could see that. He would joke and laugh like in the old days. But sometimes his laugh would die out, and he would look off into the distance.

Hector's father told his family not to worry. "Men always act like this after a war," he said. "Hector remembers his friends who died in battle. He feels sorrow, because he is still alive and able to laugh."

Mr. Martinez knew this from personal experience. He had served in the United States Army during an earlier war. He was very proud of that fact.

Hector, Jr., had been wounded early in January, during **Operation Cedar Falls**. It was late in March

---

People and Terms to Know

Operation Cedar Falls—U.S. Army code name for an attack on the "Iron Triangle," a part of South Vietnam where it was believed the enemy had a headquarters. The attack took place in January 1967.

before they let him go home. He was in a wheelchair. He had at least a year of **physical therapy** ahead of him. But at last he was home.

Hector soon discovered that home was not the same old place. His sister Marisa and his father fought all the time. Mr. Martinez complained about Marisa's long hair and colorful clothes. Mrs. Martinez just tried to keep the peace.

Dr. King urged young men not to register for Selective Service.

The Martinez family usually gathered in the living room after dinner to watch the late evening news. They did this on April 4, just a few days after Hector got home.

That night's news showed Dr. Martin Luther King, Jr., the leader of the African-American civil rights movement since the 1950s. He was speaking out against the war in Vietnam. Dr. King urged young men not to register for **Selective Service**. The speech made Mr. Martinez furious.

People and Terms to Know

physical therapy—method of healing damaged bones and muscles through massage, exercise, and other medically-planned physical activities.

Selective Service—department of the United States government that signed up young men for military duty. All young men had to register at their 18th birthday, so that they could be called up (drafted) at any time.

"How dare he criticize our country like that!" he yelled. "It's an insult to our boys in uniform! He's a filthy traitor!"

Mrs. Martinez tried to calm her husband down. "Now, honey," she said, "you know that's unfair. A lot of good people are against the war."

"Almost all my teachers think it's wrong," added Marisa. "They say that most people in Vietnam don't even want us there."

Mr. Martinez turned on her. "Let me get this straight. I'm paying for my daughter to be educated by a bunch of *communists?* Well, I don't think so! That college of yours is going to hear from me!"

Throughout this argument, Hector, Jr., said nothing. He kept saying nothing, night after night, even though the family arguments about Vietnam continued. Dr. King's speech had started similar arguments all over America.

On Saturday, April 15, the news showed huge crowds of protesters in the streets. Thousands of protesters carried huge banners with slogans like "PEACE NOW," "NO MORE U.S. BOMBS," and "GET U.S. OUT OF VIETNAM."

"They ought to lock every one of those creeps up," declared Mr. Martinez. "Let me tell you, we didn't fight and die so these **draft dodgers** could drag our country's honor through the mud."

They watched as an American helicopter, with all its guns blazing, attacked a jungle village.

Hector, Jr., continued to say nothing. Meanwhile, the pictures on the screen changed to the war itself. They watched as an American helicopter, with all its guns blazing, attacked a jungle village. Hector shuddered.

The news shifted to events at home, then to weather and sports. Mr. Martinez calmed down. Then, toward the end of the program, Vietnam came up again. A television **commentator** was saying that the leaders of the United States Army were not doing a good job running the war.

Mr. Martinez exploded again. "Listen to that!" he said angrily. "My very own son almost lost his

---

People and Terms to Know

draft dodgers—young men who did not register with the Selective Service in order to avoid going to war.

commentator—person on the radio or television news who comments, or talks about, the news of the day. He or she does this in a serious way that makes people think about an issue or topic.

▲

Anti-war protesters gather at the Capitol in Washington, D.C.

life over there. And now this communist is telling us we might lose! They ought to arrest this guy too. Don't you think so, Hector?"

For a long moment Hector was lost in his memories. "No, sir, I don't," he finally replied. "You can't arrest a guy for telling the truth."

His answer shocked Mr. Martinez into silence.

"I mean, it was like the man said," Hector explained nervously. (He wasn't used to talking back to his father.) "In fact, it was a lot worse than he said. Take Operation Cedar Falls for example.

"The area in question was what they call the Iron Triangle. It was where our officers thought the communists had their South Vietnam headquarters. So they decided to destroy it.

"Keep in mind we're talking about only 210 square miles. That's around one-sixth the size of our smallest state, Rhode Island—I looked it up. So right after New Year's we started sending B-52s over, dropping bombs. We bombed them for eight straight days—we're talking hundreds of tons of bombs.

"Meanwhile, we were moving into place— about 30,000 fighting men, plus support troops. We all moved in with our guns firing nonstop. After us came the bulldozers, mowing down everything in their path. They lifted in some of the bulldozers with these huge cranes. It was the invasion of the giant machines."

His father nodded his head. "That's what you have to do in a war," he said. "You destroyed the enemy's headquarters, right?"

"Sure," said Hector. "We found hundreds of underground tunnels and filled them in. We captured their weapons and even their secret supplies of rice. Actually, I don't remember that part, because I got blown up somewhere in there. I don't even know who blew me up, one of our guys or one of theirs."

There was another long silence. "War is never pretty," Mr. Martinez said at last. "But you still do your duty."

"We did that, sir," Hector replied. "And look what happened. We lost hundreds of men. We spent millions of dollars. We destroyed everything in our path. Then, our leaders just ordered us to pull out. You see, we didn't have enough men to hold the area.

"So—we lost hundreds of good men. We burned up millions of dollars. We blasted the jungle into desert. Then we left. I guess we did our duty."

Mr. Martinez didn't say anything. He sighed. Then he got up and walked out of the room.

Marisa turned to her brother. "Was Papa right about the protesters?" she asked. "I mean, do they make you mad?"

"Sometimes they do," replied Hector. "Over in 'Nam, you know, the communists use those protests against you. They show pictures to their prisoners, and say 'Look here, your own people are on our side.' So naturally that makes me feel bad.

"But if a person just says to my face, 'I don't like the war,' I usually say, 'Hey, man. I'm with you on that one. Believe me, you would have liked it a lot less if you'd been there.'"

QUESTIONS TO CONSIDER

1. Why do you think the Vietnam War was referred to as a "living room war"?

2. Why did Operation Cedar Falls change Hector's attitude about the Vietnam War?

3. How did some Americans show that they were against the war?

4. How did the U.S. enemy in Vietnam use the anti-war protests in the United States?

5. What is your opinion about protesting a war your nation is fighting?

Witness to the Tet Offensive

BY MARIANNE McCOMB

Lila, who had lived her whole life in the United States, went to Vietnam out of a sense of duty to her country. To convince her parents to let her go, she reminded them that **President Johnson** had said the war would be over soon. She strengthened her argument by saying that this was her chance to put her training as a nurse to good use. Lila's parents gave their blessing, although Lila was only twenty-one and had graduated from nursing school just one month ago.

People and Terms to Know

President Johnson—Lyndon Johnson (1908–1973), 36th President of the United States (1963–1969). During his presidency American forces became bogged down in the Vietnam War. At home, he started a different war—against poverty.

The first enlisted women in the U.S. Air Force arrive in Vietnam in 1967.

So, Lila packed her bags and left home. The six weeks she spent in training flew by. She received her orders to ship out to Vietnam on December 1, 1968. She was assigned to a military hospital in Saigon, the capital of South Vietnam.

The Saigon hospital was quite small, and many of its buildings were little more than huts. The "recovery ward" she worked in was really just a room with a roof and a window.

Even though everything was so different, Lila adjusted very quickly. She learned how to dress a wound, splint a broken limb, and soothe soldiers who were feverish or homesick or just lonely for a friendly face.

Almost every night, Lila wrote a letter home. She wanted her parents to know that she was okay, that the work was interesting, and that she had made some friends. In one letter, Lila wrote that she was looking forward to the celebration of **Tet**, which would take place on January 31.

People and Terms to Know

Tet—Vietnamese term for the lunar (LOO•nar) new year. In the United States most people celebrate a solar (SOH•lar) new year based upon Earth moving fully around the Sun.

Sometime after 3:00 A.M. on the night before Tet, Lila sat down at her desk and began writing a letter. At around 3:30, she heard

That first peek out the window was, for her, the worst moment of the attack.

what sounded like firecracker bursts a short distance away. A moment later, the firecracker sounds were louder, as if they were moving her way. Lila decided to take a look out the hospital window.

That first peek out the window was, for her, the worst moment of the attack that would come to be called the "Tet offensive." In the horrible days that followed the attack on Saigon—days of screaming soldiers and blood-soaked sheets and nurses crying as they covered the faces of one dead man after another—Lila kept picturing the scene from the window. She couldn't stop thinking about it.

That night, when Lila had looked outside, the first thing she noticed was the light. The moon was so bright that it cast a milky glow over everything it touched. For a few seconds, Lila did nothing more than gaze out the window and wonder how it could be so *bright* in the middle of the night.

Because of the strange glow of the moon, Lila began to feel a little unsettled. She wasn't *nervous* exactly, but she knew that something wasn't exactly right. So she did what she had been doing since arriving in Saigon, when she was feeling strange. She turned her head ever so slightly and let her eyes wander down the street toward the U.S. **embassy**. To look quickly would mean that she was truly afraid, and she certainly wasn't that scared.

As she shifted her eyes toward the embassy, Lila saw one or two other things, besides the moonlight, that seemed a little strange. Over to the right, there was a man in the street who was just standing there, with his hands over his ears. A little further down there were a couple of jeeps parked any old way, as if the drivers had been in a terrible hurry. There was a pool of what looked like black oil spreading from a puddle on the walkway leading up to the embassy. Lila knew that oil was never on the walkway to the embassy. Now she was *sure* that something was wrong.

At last, Lila's eyes reached the wall that surrounded the main building of the embassy. She told

---

People and Terms to Know

embassy—official residence and offices of an ambassador in a foreign country.

herself that she would make her eyes climb the wall slowly. At the top of the wall, she would see the embassy building, as always, and it would mean that everything was fine. But before her eyes could travel even halfway up the wall, Lila realized that everything was not *fine*, that in fact everything was pretty much the opposite of *fine*.

The top part of the wall that surrounded the embassy, Lila saw, was blown to bits. It was crumbling. There was a jagged hole the size of an army jeep. Dozens of Vietcong soldiers were heaving themselves *through* the hole, one after another. The soldiers, with their guns held high, rushed toward the front door of the embassy itself.

Suddenly the cracks and booms of the fireworks, which Lila now understood was the sound of gunfire, grew sharper and louder. Mixed in was the sound of people screaming and sirens wailing in the distance. Somewhere behind her, she could hear a radio operator screaming into his headset. "The North Vietnamese are attacking Saigon!" he kept yelling. "And they're hitting a lot of other cities too! They're everywhere, everywhere!"

▲

Black smoke covers areas of Saigon from attacks by the Vietcong
during Tet in 1968.

Lila closed her eyes and turned away from the window. Her mind was racing with thoughts of what was to come. Already, she could hear the screams for help, the doctors barking out orders, and the small rooms of the hospital filling with pain and fear. The Vietnam War, Lila realized, had come at last to Saigon, to her own back door.

The Vietnam War, Lila realized, had come at last to Saigon, to her own back door.

*　　*　　*

February 3, 1968
Saigon

Dear Mom and Dad,

I hope you haven't worried too much because you haven't heard from me in a few days. I started writing you a letter a few days ago, but I threw it out. That's because everything has changed.

Even now I have only a minute to write. I've been working around the clock for the last three days. I'm not sure how much you've heard in the U.S., but I wanted to let you know that I'm okay.

Three nights ago, on the evening of Tet, a fifteen-man suicide squad blew a hole in the wall around the U. S. embassy in Saigon. I watched it happen. It was horrible, Mom, worse than you can ever imagine. There were so many bleeding people, and so many frightened children.

Later, we learned that 84,000 enemy troops were involved in this Tet offensive. In an attempt to bring about a quick end to the war, communist troops attacked every major city in South Vietnam. Saigon was just one of them. In all, five U.S. marines, four South Vietnamese officials, and fifteen Vietcong were killed in the gunfight outside the embassy. But that night, it felt like thousands.

I think, Mom and Dad, that I won't be coming home anytime soon. Up until Tet, Americans were saying that the war was just about won. But now I know for a fact that's not true. The North Vietnamese lost thousands of soldiers during Tet, but they're *not* giving up. They're going to keep fighting and fighting and won't stop until *we* stop. Tet proves that. I guess Americans would do the same thing if a foreign country had its armies on our soil. So those rumors that you've been hearing that we've won the war are false. We haven't won anything at all.

Love,
Lila

Lila turned out to be right. The United States continued to send its troops into Vietnam for another five years, until 1973. In fact, the Vietnam War turned out to be America's longest military conflict. The Tet Offensive occurred when Lyndon Johnson was president. One reason why Johnson decided not to run for reelection was that America was not winning the war.

But the surprise attack had raised doubts for Americans, and it's hard to win a war without confidence.

Later, many people saw the Tet Offensive as the turning point of the war. Following Tet, things went downhill for the United States. People felt this way even though the Tet Offensive was a military defeat for the communists. They won no cities and lost 45,000 soldiers. South Vietnam lost 2,300 and the United States lost even fewer—1,100. But the surprise attack had raised doubts for Americans, and it's hard to win a war without confidence.

When American troops left Vietnam in 1973, **Richard Nixon** was president. His presidency was also marked by years of military failure in Vietnam. In 1975, South Vietnam surrendered to North Vietnam. By then, the United States had yet another president in office.

Saigon, the city in which Lila and so many other Americans had served their country, was renamed. It was now called **Ho Chi Minh** City, after the North Vietnamese leader.

QUESTIONS TO CONSIDER

1. Why did Lila volunteer to go to Vietnam?

2. What effect did the Tet Offensive have on Lila?

3. Why do you think North Vietnamese forces did not give up, even after suffering great losses in the Tet Offensive?

4. Why do you think Lila always looked to the U.S. embassy first when she "felt strange"?

People and Terms to Know

Richard Nixon—(1913–1994) 37th president of the United States (1969–1974). Nixon increased U.S. military involvement in Southeast Asia and helped begin communication with communist China. He resigned from office in 1974.

Ho Chi Minh (hoh chee mihn)—(1890–1969) national hero of Vietnam. He was the leader of the Vietnamese communists against three foreign armies from the 1940s to the 1970s: the Japanese, the French, and the Americans.

In a speech President Lyndon B. Johnson gave on April 7, 1965, he spoke about why he believed the United States should continue to fight in Vietnam.

"We are there because we have a promise to keep. Since 1954 every American president has offered support to the people of South Vietnam. We have helped to build, and we have helped to defend. Thus, over many years, we have made a national pledge to help South Vietnam defend its independence.

And I intend to keep that promise. . . .

We are also there to strengthen world order. Around the globe, from Berlin to Thailand, are people whose well-being rests, in part, on the belief that they can count on us if they are ever attacked. To leave Vietnam to its fate would shake the confidence of all these people in the value of an American commitment and in the value of America's word. The result would be increased unrest and instability, and even wider war."

The Vietnam Veterans Memorial

BY STEPHEN CURRIE

Men don't cry, my daddy always told me. I expect I was about four years old when I gave up crying for good. I didn't cry when I broke my arm. I didn't cry when my dog died. Heck, I didn't even cry when Grandma passed on. I stood at the funeral parlor, tall and straight and dry-eyed. I had nothing but scorn for the sobbing people around me.

Oh, I was a strong one. After high school, I enlisted in the army and got shipped to Vietnam. My big sister Susan cried over me. "What if you don't come back?" she asked. She cried, but I didn't. I wouldn't because men don't cry. "I'll be back," I told her.

Of course I'd be back, I thought. Only the weak got shot, right?

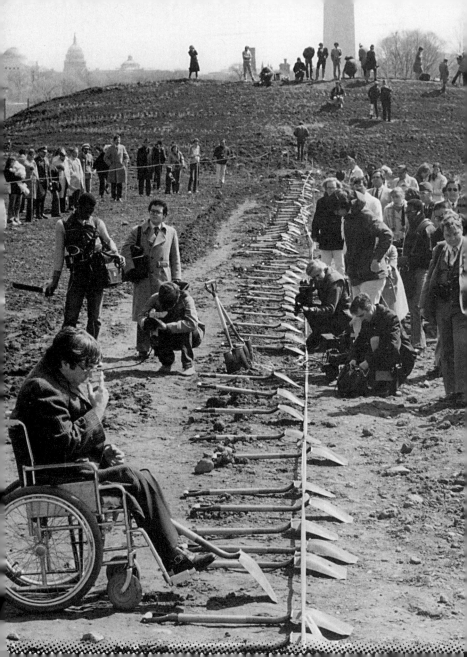

*   *   *

"**O**h, my," murmured Susan McWilliams.

Shivering in the autumn chill, she stared at the shiny black granite wall, which stretched across Washington's **National Mall** like two arms of a gigantic *V*. The **Vietnam Veterans Memorial**, they called it. Cut into the hard stone of the wall, Susan knew, were names. There were nearly 60,000 in all: all Americans who had lost their lives in the Vietnam War.

Half the world had come to Washington for the dedication of the new memorial.

Gently she touched her brother Darrell's sleeve. They had stayed close together in this crowd of Vietnam veterans and their loved ones. It seemed that half the world had come to Washington for the dedication of the new memorial. "What do you think?" she asked.

Darrell hardly seemed to hear. His eyes stared intently at the wall ahead.

People and Terms to Know

National Mall—federal park area in downtown Washington, D.C., that connects many public buildings and monuments.

Vietnam Veterans Memorial—monument to the dead of the Vietnam War, unveiled in Washington, D.C., on November 13, 1982.

"We'll go see the wall close up after the ceremony," said Susan. She had insisted on bringing Darrell today, hoping that seeing the memorial would help heal some old wounds. With any luck, she thought, that would prove to be the right decision. Sliding her arm around the small of his back, she followed Darrell's gaze.

It was strange how a simple wall could be so moving. The memorial was gentle and calm. Susan had read that it had been designed by a woman named **Maya Lin**. In America's last three wars, the nation had fought against Japan, Korea, and Vietnam—all countries in East Asia. Now an American of East Asian background was responsible for this powerful monument. To Susan, that seemed only right—like it was part of the healing America needed.

The shiny black surface of the wall was reflective, like a pool of still water. It glistened and reflected the light of the afternoon sun. Susan couldn't imagine a more peaceful place to honor the dead. What will it be like, she wondered, to see the wall close up, to read the names carved into the surface?

People and Terms to Know

Maya Lin—(b. 1959) architect who designed the Vietnam Veterans Memorial.

A tear trickled from the corner of her eye. She shivered again, this time not entirely from the cold.

* * *

In 'Nam, I discovered that being strong didn't mean much. One of the strongest, bravest men I knew took a bullet two weeks into our tour of duty. Another blew to pieces when he stepped on a land mine. Then there was my buddy Andy Garza, killed on that terrible day in '68.

I came back from 'Nam, all right. But in a way, I never really returned.

Each time, I blinked back the tears, told myself I didn't feel a thing. Like Daddy always said, men don't cry.

But, you know, even now some nights I dream about being in Vietnam. I dream about bullets that just miss me. I dream about bombs and wounded men screaming for help. Most of all, I dream about Garza. I wake in a cold sweat. Nights like that, Vietnam seems more real to me than real life.

I came back from 'Nam, all right. But in a way, I never really returned.

* * *

The ceremony had been brief, and now the crowds surged toward the monument. Susan and Darrell were swept forward along with thousands of others. Some wore medals. Others carried flags. "Never Again," read one homemade sign. "Thank You, Veterans," said another. A third read simply, "Welcome Home."

"Welcome Home." Susan's eyes began to tear again, as she recalled those dark days of the early '70s. She reached for her brother's hand.

*   *   *

The weird thing was when I came home for good, back in '71.

Everything had gotten so political by then. Daddy was furious that we weren't winning the war. Susan was protesting against it. No one paid much attention to us soldiers. People just changed the subject when you started talking about 'Nam. They didn't want to talk about what you'd done or what you'd seen. It was like I'd never been there.

So I shut up about it. I got back to real life. I ran away from the war and my memories, and it worked. After a while I began to think maybe I'd never been there after all. But of course that wasn't possible on those nights when I'd wake up in terror from the dreams.

I had always planned on looking up Garza's family. He was a good friend and a good man. But I never did. The way things were, it seemed like his family might not care to have some veteran like me bothering them.

*   *   *

The names reach out and grab you, thought Susan.

She and Darrell were at the base of the wall. Nearby, two burly men sobbed in each other's arms. A woman hugged a teenage boy. A scrawny man with gray hair gently ran his finger across a name. His face was reflected in the granite. Susan saw sadness in his eyes. Then she saw something else—pride.

Look at all those names, thought Susan. She did not understand all her feelings at that moment. So many had died. They included husbands, fathers, brothers, and sons. Susan touched the name nearest her. She knew nothing about the man it belonged to, but even so she felt a sudden connection to him.

It is important to have people know this man's name, Susan thought. It is important to talk about him and what he did. It will help heal the wounds—mine, my brother's, those of all who come here. It will help heal our nation's wounds.

For eleven years I'd been running away from 'Nam.

"Darrell?" Susan cleared her throat. "When you came home in '71—I thought the war was a bad idea. I still think so. But that had nothing to do with you. You did the best you could, and in my own way I was proud of you. I'm prouder today." Her voice broke. "Welcome home, little brother."

*   *   *

I hadn't wanted to come to the Wall, you know. For eleven years I'd been running away from 'Nam. The war had seen too much waste, too much death, and too little healing. There were even people dying here in the states—take a look at what happened at **Kent State** the year before I came home.

I agreed to let Susan take me, but privately I promised that it wouldn't affect me.

People and Terms to Know

Kent State—university in Ohio where, in 1970, four students were killed by the U.S. National Guard during protests against the Vietnam War.

But I was wrong. Now that I'd seen it, somehow I felt whole again, as if a missing piece of myself had somehow been found. And there was something I knew I had to do.

"This is the one," I said. I reached up to touch the name engraved in the shiny black granite: Andrew A. Garza.

To me he was just Andy. To me, he was my friend, my buddy.

For a moment I stayed there, Susan's hand on my shoulder, my hand on Andy's name, thinking thoughts I did not know I knew how to think.

* * *

Darrell had been there for several minutes, Susan was sure. His body shook silently, his fingers still pressed against the familiar name carved so neatly into the Wall. "Are you all right?" she asked anxiously.

"Daddy was wrong," said Darrell in a voice that rang with sorrow and triumph at the same time.

Susan frowned. "Wrong about what?"

Without lifting his fingers from the stone, Darrell turned. His face was streaked with tears, tears that shone and glistened like the Wall itself.

"Men *do* cry," he said.

QUESTIONS TO CONSIDER

1. According to Darrell, what was especially hard about serving in Vietnam?

2. What kind of wounds does Susan hope to heal by bringing Darrell to the memorial?

3. What is Susan's reaction to the Wall? How do you know?

4. What does Darrell mean when he says, "I came back from 'Nam, all right. But in a way, I never really returned"?

5. In what ways does Darrell change in the story? How and why do the changes take place?

The Vietnam Veterans Memorial carries the names of more than 58,000 Americans dead or missing in the war.

Sources

An American Family Learns of Pearl Harbor
by Walter Hazen

The narrator, his family, and his friends are fictional, although they are based on people who lived at the time and whom the author recalls firsthand. In his additional research, he relied mainly on the comprehensive *Day of Infamy* by Walter Lord (New York: Henry Holt & Company, 1957).

Rosie the Riveter *by Judith Conaway*

Hannah and her family are fictional, but they are based on real people: the author's mother and grandmother worked in industrial plants in California during World War II, and her father served in the U.S. Navy in the South Pacific. More information on this extraordinary time can be found in two excellent history collections: *Women's America: Refocusing the Past*, edited by Linda K. Kerber and Jane De Hart-Mathews (Oxford: Oxford University Press, 1987) and *Looking for America: The People's History*, Vol. II., edited by Stanley L. Kutler (W.W. Norton, 1979).

Navajo Code Talkers *by Judith Lloyd Yero*

The characters in the story are fictional, but all of the information about the code talkers is historically accurate. One fascinating source of information on them is *The Navajo Code Talkers* by Doris A. Paul (Philadelphia: Dorrance and Company, 1973). Readers interested in this topic might also like to know that there's a "G. I. Joe" action figure of a code talker who speaks both English and Navajo.

D–Day *by Stephen Feinstein*

Roger Curran, and the rest of the soldiers in the story are all fictional characters. The planning, strategy, and execution of the D-Day invasion have been the subject of countless books. Of these, the author mainly used Stephen E. Ambrose's highly-detailed *D-Day, June 6, 1944: The Climactic Battle of World War II* (New York: Simon & Schuster, 1994).

The Atomic Bomb *by Dee Masters*

The dropping of the atomic bombs on Japan is one of the most written-about events of the 20th century. John Hersey's classic *Hiroshima* (New York: Vintage, 1989) is a journalistic account that reads like a novel and has moved generations of readers.

Heading Toward "Heartbreak" *by Walter Hazen*

Captain Newman, Phil, Mark and the narrator are fictional characters. The only real person appearing in the story is the commanding general of the 2nd Division, who is not mentioned by name. Readers interested in this often over-looked conflict may wish to check out *Korea: The First War We Lost* by Bevin Alexander (New York: Hippocene Books, 1986) and the recent *The Korean War* by Brian Catchpole (New York: Carroll & Graf, 2000).

U.S. Army *versus* **McCarthy** *by Stephen Currie*

Gripping historical accounts of this notorious era can be found in Robert Goldston's *The American Nightmare: Senator Joseph R. McCarthy and the Politics of Hate* (Indianapolis: Bobbs-Merrill, 1973) and Ellen Schrecker's *Many Are the Crimes: McCarthyism in America* (Boston: Little, Brown 1998). The couple following the hearings on television are fictional, but the people they watched, and their words, are entirely real.

The Soviets Launch *Sputnik*
by Judith Conaway

Though the main character of this story is fictional, Bobby's feelings reflect those of many Americans of the time. For more information about the United States space program and the "space race" against the Soviet Union in the 1950s, visit NASA's official web site at **history.nasa.gov**. Select the "History" section when you get to the site.

Cuban Missile Crisis *by Danny Miller*

The Rosen family and Mr. Larson are fictional characters. As government documents continue to be declassified, there are more interesting studies available of what went on behind the scenes during the Cuban missile crisis. Three good sources are: *The Missiles of October* by Robert Smith Thompson (New York: Simon & Schuster, 1992); *Eyeball to Eyeball: The Inside Story of the Cuban Missile Crisis* by Dino A. Brugioni (New York: Random House, 1990, 1991); and *The Crisis Years: Kennedy and Khrushchev, 1960–1963* by Michael R. Beschloss (New York: HarperCollins Publishers, 1991).

Jungle Warfare *by Brian J. Mahoney*

The narrator and his friends Tyrone and Mikey are fictional characters. However, their feelings and experiences reflect those of Vietnam War soldiers as reported in journalist Michael Herr's powerful *Dispatches* (New York: Random House, 1968). Other important books on this war include Frances Fitzgerald's *Fire in the Lake* (New York: Vintage, 1972) and Wallace Terry's *Bloods: An Oral History of the Vietnam War by Black Veterans* (New York: Ballantine, 1985).

Black Soldiers in Vietnam *by Judith Lloyd Yero*

The narrator is a fictional character, but his thoughts are drawn from a number of different articles by, and interviews with, African Americans who served in Vietnam. The author recommends *Vietnam Shadows: The War, Its Ghosts, and Its Legacy* by Arnold R. Isaacs (Baltimore: The Johns Hopkins University Press, 1997) and *The Vietnam Reader*, edited by Steward O'Nan (New York: Anchor Books/Doubleday, 1998).

Witness to the Tet Offensive *by Marianne McComb*
The characters in the story that lived through the Tet offensive are entirely fictional. However, what Lila experienced during those days was real to many people. Those interested in reading more on the subject should try to find *Vietnam: The Valor and the Sorrow* by Thomas D. Boettcher (Boston: Little, Brown 1985).

A "Living Room War" *by Judith Conaway*
The main character and his family are fictional. But Dr. Martin Luther King, Jr.'s speech, and the anti-war protests really did take place. The source for the detailed account of "Operation Cedar Falls" is Bernard B. Fall's "Unrepentant, Unyielding: An Interview with Viet Cong Prisoners" in *The New Republic*, February 4, 1967. The article has been reprinted in *Reporting Vietnam: American Journalism, 1959–1975* (Library of America, 2000).

Vietnam Veterans Memorial *by Stephen Currie*
Darrel and Susan are fictional characters, but their experiences reflect those of many visitors to the Vietnam Veterans Memorial. The years following the opening of "The Wall" to the public in 1982 saw the appearance of several thoughtful history books that revisited the aftermath of the Vietnam War. Of these, the author relied on *To Heal a Nation* by Jan C. Scruggs and Joel L. Swerdlow (New York: Harper and Row, 1985) and *Shrapnel in the Heart* by Laura Palmer (New York: Random House, 1987).

Glossary of People and Terms to Know

aircraft carrier—warship with a flat deck from which fighter planes can take off and land. Aircraft carriers are necessary because fighting planes often cannot hold enough fuel for long flights.

air-raid drill—practice exercise to prepare for an attack by planes dropping bombs.

AK-47—rifle used by communist forces in Vietnam.

Ali—Muhammed Ali, African-American heavyweight boxing champion who refused to be drafted into the military during the Vietnam War.

Allies—The Allies were the United States, Great Britain, the Soviet Union (Russia), and other nations that fought against the Axis powers during World War II.

allies—countries joined together for a common purpose, such as defeating an enemy.

ambush—planned surprise attack on moving enemy troops.

Anglos—informal term for white Americans who are not of Hispanic descent.

assembly line—arrangement in which products are put together in stages as they pass from worker to worker or machine to machine, often on a conveyor belt.

atomic bomb—type of explosive that kills people not only with its blast, but also with radiation. An atomic bomb has hundreds of times more killing power than a conventional bomb.

Axis Powers—Germany, Japan, Italy, and the nations that fought against the Allies during World War II.

Battle of Midway—naval battle that took place near the Midway Islands in the central Pacific, on June 3–6, 1942. It was an important early victory for the United States in the war against Japan.

blockade—use of ships or troops to prevent movement into and out of a port or region controlled by an enemy.

boot camp—camp where people who have just joined the military go for basic training.

bunker—strongly built shelter, especially one built underground.

canteen—club where soldiers are entertained.

Castro, Fidel—born in 1926, political leader of Cuba since 1959. The revolution he led that year made Cuba the first communist state in the same part of the world as the United States.

casualties—people killed or wounded.

Charlie—nickname for the United States' enemy in the Vietnam War.

civil war—war fought within a single country by its own people.

code talker—U.S. Marine in the Pacific during World War II whose duty was to transmit important messages in code.

Cold War—(1945–1991) period of conflict—but rarely all-out war—between the democratic nations of the world, led by the United States, and the communist nations, led by the Soviet Union.

commentator—journalist who offers opinions about the news of the day in a serious way that makes people think about an issue or topic.

communism—economic and political system based on government ownership of property and businesses and a one-party government.

communists—people who believe the government should control the whole economy in order to share wealth throughout the community. The Soviet Union was the leading communist country until it broke apart in 1991.

Cuba—small island country in the Caribbean Sea, off the southern coast of Florida.

dap—complicated way of shaking hands or greeting one another. It was started by African-American troops.

D-Day—(from the word "designated" plus "day") June 6, 1944, the day chosen for the Allied invasion of Normandy, France, to begin.

dictatorship—absolute rule of a country by one strong central power, with no guarantees for the rights of the citizens.

Diné (dee•NAY)—term used by the Navajo to describe their own people.

draft dodgers—young men who did not register with the Selective Service in order to avoid going to war.

embassy—official residence and offices of an ambassador in a foreign country.

Enemyway—Navajo ceremony for men who return from battle. It is designed to free them from the spirits of the enemies and the bad memories of battle, bringing them back into harmony with nature.

English Channel—body of water that separates England from France.

enlisted—signed up voluntarily to serve in the army, navy, or other branch of the armed services.

fallout shelter—underground place built to protect people from the effects of nuclear bombs. Fallout is the name for tiny pieces of material that fall from the sky, often well after a blast. They can cause serious illness or death.

foxhole—hole dug for protection in combat.

French Indochina—area of southeast Asia once controlled by France. Today the region includes the nations of Laos (LAH•ohs), Cambodia, and Vietnam. See the map on page 26.

fuselage (FYOO•suh•lahj)—body of an airplane, without its wings, tail, or engines.

Geronimo—(c. 1829–1909) Native American who led Apaches to escape their reservations in Arizona in the late 1800s.

GIs—abbreviation standing for "general issue" or "government issue." It refers to soldiers of the U.S. Army.

Great Depression—period of terrible economic trouble that began in 1930 and lasted up until World War II. At one point one out of every four American workers was unemployed.

Guadalcanal—one of the Solomon Islands in the South Pacific, where several battles were fought between August 1942 and February 1943. The United States and its allies defeated Japanese forces, but at the cost of thousands of lives.

Hanoi—capital of North Vietnam, where the leaders of its government and military were based.

Hatfield, Mark—(b. 1922) World War II veteran, governor of Oregon from 1958 to 1968 and U.S. senator from Oregon from 1969 to 1997.

Hayes, Ira—(1923–1955) Pima Indian Marine who was one of the men in the famous picture of the American flag being raised on Iwo Jima.

hearings—public meetings to determine the truth about a serious situation. In 1954, hearings were held in the Senate about charges that Senator Joseph McCarthy had made that several Army officials were communists.

Hirohito (HEER•roh•HEE•toh)—(1901–1989) emperor of Japan during World War II and the postwar years.

Ho Chi Minh (hoh chee mihn)—national hero of Vietnam. Leader of the Vietnamese communists against three foreign armies from the 1940s to the 1970s: the Japanese, the French, and the Americans.

Iwo Jima (EE•whoh•JEE•muh)—island in the western Pacific that was under Japanese control until 1945. The U.S. wanted it as a base for planes bombing Japan. The two sides fought for nearly a month before the United States captured the island.

Johnson, Lyndon—(1908–1973) 36th President of the United States, (1963–1969). During his presidency American forces became bogged down in the Vietnam War. At home, he started a different war—against poverty.

Kaesong—town on Korea's west coast. It is situated at the 38th parallel, which divides North and South Korea.

Kennedy, John F.—(1917–1963), 35th President of the United States (1961–1963); assassinated in November 1963, the year after the Cuban Missile Crisis.

Kennedy, Robert F.—(1925–1968) brother of President John Kennedy and U.S. attorney general (1961–1964), who led a major fight against organized crime. Later a senator from New York (1965–1968), Robert Kennedy was assassinated in 1968 as he ran for president.

Kent State—university in Ohio where, in 1970, four students were killed by the U.S. National Guard during protests against the Vietnam War.

King Jr., Dr. Martin Luther—(1929–1968) minister who led the African-American civil rights movement in the United States from the mid-1950s until his assassination in 1968.

Korean War—(1950–1953) war in which North Korea and China fought South Korea, which was supported by an international fighting force that was largely American. It was the first war the United States fought against communist countries.

Khrushchev (kroosh•CHOF), **Nikita**—(1894–1971), leader of the Soviet Union from 1953 to 1964 during the height of the Cold War.

land mine—small bomb or similar device buried in the ground and set to explode when stepped on or run over by a vehicle. Land mines left over from earlier wars are responsible for thousands of deaths and injuries each year worldwide.

LCT—short for "landing craft, tank." A tank-carrying landing craft, it was much smaller than an LST.

Lin, Maya—(b. 1959) architect who designed the Vietnam Veterans Memorial.

LST—short for "landing ship, tank." These ships were made to carry battle tanks and heavy rolling equipment over sea to battle areas and unload directly onto the shore.

MacArthur, Douglas—(1880–1964) American general who lost the Philippines to Japan in World War II, but later retook them. In the 1950s he was the leader of all United Nations forces in the Korean War.

machetes (muh•SHET•eez)—long knives used for cutting vegetation.

Marshall Islands—small group of islands in the central Pacific Ocean. They were captured by the United States and its allies during February 1944.

McCarthy, Joseph—(1909–1957) Wisconsin senator first elected in 1946. Beginning in 1950, he accused many people in the federal government of being traitors with little proof. After hearings in 1954, the Senate punished McCarthy for his actions, and he faded from public view.

Milwaukee Braves—baseball team now called the Atlanta Braves that played in Milwaukee in the 1950s.

missing in action—(MIA) official term for a military person who cannot be accounted for after a battle.

missionary—religious teacher who works to spread his or her religion to a new country or people where it is not widely known or practiced.

mortar—short cannon for firing shells high into the air.

mushroom cloud—cloud produced by an atomic bomb explosion. It resembles a giant mushroom in shape.

National Mall—federal park area in downtown Washington, D.C., that connects many public buildings and monuments.

Navajo—group of Native Americans living in the southwestern United States. A code based on the Navajo language was very important to the United States in its fight against the Japanese in World War II.

newsreels—short films covering recent news events. Newsreels were shown in theaters, usually before the main movie.

Nixon, Richard—(1913–1994) 37th president of the United States (1969–1974). Nixon increased U.S. military involvement in Southeast Asia and helped begin communication with communist China. He resigned from office in 1974.

Normandy—region in northwestern France along the Atlantic coast. It was where the Allies began retaking France from German forces.

nuclear weapons—weapons powered by splitting atoms, the smallest building blocks of matter. When this happens, huge amounts of energy are released, and entire cities can be wiped out by one bomb.

Oahu—third largest and most important of the Hawaiian Islands. Honolulu, Hawaii's largest city, is located on Oahu.

occupation force—foreign soldiers controlling a country. The American military ran Japan from 1945 to 1952. The aim was to create a democratic government in Japan and help it rebuild after the war.

offensive—for the purpose of attacking rather than defending.

Okinawa—island near Japan where one of the bloodiest fights of World War II happened. 5,000 marines died in the landings alone.

Omaha Beach—one of five beaches along the Normandy coast code-named by the Allies. D-Day invasion forces landed here and on Utah, Gold, Juno, and Sword beaches.

Operation Cedar Falls—U.S. Army code name for an attack on the "Iron Triangle," a part of South Vietnam where it was believed the enemy had a headquarters. The attack took place in January, 1967.

Operation Overlord—Allied invasion of France, which had been under Germany's rule for four years. It was led by U.S. General Dwight D. Eisenhower

Oval Office—president's office in the White House, his home in Washington, D.C.

Paris—capital of France. From 1940 until 1944 it was controlled by German forces.

Pearl Harbor—major U.S. naval base near Honolulu, Hawaii. Japanese planes made a surprise attack on it on December 7, 1941, that brought the United States into World War II.

physical therapy—method of healing damaged bones and muscles through massage, exercise, and other medically-planned physical activities.

pillboxes—small, low concrete structures on which machine guns and anti-tank weapons are placed.

platoon—military group of about 45 soldiers commanded by a lieutenant.

point of order—question as to whether the discussion going on in a meeting is allowed by the rules. When someone calls for a point of order, discussion must stop while the chairman decides the question. McCarthy used this rule over and over to interrupt others.

Presley, Elvis—(1935–1977) major music and movie star in the 1950s and 1960s. To this day, Presley is called the "King" of rock 'n roll.

Punchbowl—dead volcanic crater near the 38th parallel. Overlooking it were hills where some of the bloodiest fights of the Korean War took place.

rations—specific amounts of food or another valuable item that is allowed to each person or family during wartime. Many everyday items were rationed during World War II so that those in the military would have enough supplies to fight.

Reds—nickname for communists.

reservation—land set aside by the U.S. government for Native American groups.

ROKs—soldiers of the Republic of Korea, or South Korea.

Roosevelt, Franklin D.—(1882–1945) 32nd president of the United States, elected first in 1932 and then three times after that. He helped the country get through both the Great Depression and most of World War II.

Rosie the Riveter—imaginary heroine used by the U.S. during World War II to encourage women to work in war industries. The song "Rosie the Riveter" was written by Redd Evans and John Jacob Loeb.

sabotage (SAB•oh•tahj)—destruction of machinery and equipment by enemy agents.

satellites—objects that orbit around a larger body in space. These objects can be man-made or natural, like a moon.

Selective Service—department of the United States government that signed up young men for military duty. All young men had to register at their 18th birthday, so that they could be called up (drafted) at any time.

siege—attempt by an army to force a city to surrender by surrounding it and cutting off supplies.

Soviet Union—short for "Union of Soviet Socialist Republics." This was an empire made up of Russia and nearby nations it controlled. The Soviet Union was formed in 1917 and broke apart in 1991.

Sputnik—first manmade object to orbit the earth. It was launched from a rocket by the Soviet Union in 1957.

State Department—U.S. government office in charge of foreign policy.

Tail-Gunner Joe—nickname given to Senator Joseph McCarthy for the heroics he was supposed to have performed during World War II.

Tet—Vietnamese term for the lunar (LOO•nar) new year. In the United States most people celebrate a solar (SOH•lar) new year based upon Earth moving fully around the Sun.

Tibetan (tih•BEHT•an)—from the Asian country of Tibet, which is now controlled by China.

Tokyo—Japan's largest city and its capital.

tour of duty—period of military service during wartime.

truce—temporary peace during wartime.

Truman, Harry—(1884–1972) 33rd president of the United States (1945–1953). He made the decision to use atomic bombs on Japan.

United Nations—or U.N., international peacekeeping organization made up of most of the nations of the world. It was founded in 1945, after the end of World War II, to promote world peace, security, and economic development.

USO—(United Service Organizations) volunteer group that provides clubs, entertainment, and other services for men and women in the U.S. armed forces.

VA hospital—hospital run by the Veterans Administration.

Van Allen radiation belt—area of high magnetism that surrounds Earth. It was discovered by American scientist James A. Van Allen.

VC—short for the Vietcong, South Vietnam Communists who fought for North Vietnam.

V-E Day—"Victory in Europe" Day on May 8, 1945. President Truman made it a national holiday after Germany surrendered on May 7.

Vietcong (vee•eht•KAHNG)— South Vietnamese Communists who, with North Vietnamese support, fought against the government of South Vietnam in the Vietnam War.

Vietnam—country in Southeast Asia. In 1954 it was divided into two countries, North Vietnam and South Vietnam. Beginning in the 1960s U.S. forces fought to protect South Vietnam from control by the North. See the map on page 26.

Vietnam Veterans Memorial— monument to the dead of the Vietnam War; unveiled in Washington, D.C., on November 13, 1982.

Vietnam War—(1955–1975) war between communist North Vietnam and South Vietnam. South Vietnam was supported by U.S. troops from 1965 until 1973 and surrendered in 1975.

V-J Day—"Victory in Japan" Day on August 15, 1945. This was the day after Japan surrendered, ending World War II.

Welch, Joseph Nye—lead lawyer for the Army in the 1954 Senate hearings into Senator McCarthy's charges of communism in the Army.

Acknowledgements

9, 15, 18, 19 Courtesy of the Library of Congress.
21 Don Hesse, 1950.
24 Courtesy of the Library of Congress.
31 American Treasures.
34, 42, 45, 54 Courtesy of the Library of Congress.
44–46, 52 *Rosie the Riveter,* Words and Music by Redd Evans and John Jacob Loeb. Copyright © 1942 (Renewed) by Music Sales Corporation (ASCAP) and Fred Ahlert Music Corporation. Copyright © 1942 (Renewed 1969) John J. Loeb Company and Music Sales Corporation. Exclusive License for John J. Loeb Company: Fred Ahlert Music Corporation. All Rights for the World excluding the United States Controlled and Administered by Famous Music Corporation. International Copyright Secured. All Rights Reserved. Reprinted by Permission.

57 Courtesy of the National Archives.
64, 73 Courtesy of the Library of Congress.
75 Courtesy of the National Archives.
77, 85 Courtesy of the Library of Congress.
93 Courtesy of the National Archives.
99, 106 Courtesy of the Library of Congress.
111 © Robert Phillips/Black Star.
120 Courtesy of the Library of Congress.
126 Courtesy of NASA.
131, 136, 145 Courtesy of the Library of Congress.
152 © AP/Wide World Photos.
157, 161, 166 Courtesy of the Library of Congress.
171 Courtesy of the National Archives.
176, 181, 188, 196 Courtesy of the Library of Congress.